CW01646750

HEROES OF 100 TESTS

From Cowdrey and the Waughs to Warne, Tendulkar and Hooper

A magnificent century by Mark Taylor in the 1989 Leeds Test. *(Gift from Ronald Cardwell)*

HEROES OF 100 TESTS

From Cowdrey and the Waughs to Warne, Tendulkar and Hooper

Kersi Meher-Homji

ROSENBERG

First Published in 2003 by Rosenberg Publishing Pty Ltd
P.O. Box 6125 Dural Delivery Centre NSW 2156 Australia
Phone (612) 9654 1502 Fax (612) 9654 1338
Email rosenbergpub@smartchat.net.au Web www.rosenbergpub.com.au

ISBN 1877058 114

Set in AGaramond 12 on 14 point
Cover by Highway 51 Design Works

Printed in China by Everbest Printing Co. Limited

Contents

Getting to grips, Tendulkar and Kapil Dev during a one-day international in Delhi. *(Courtesy G.E. Features)*

Foreword
by Peter Roebuck

Everyone contributes to cricket in his own way. Some men dominate the headlines with their deeds and others write the stories that hold the attention of the reader. Some men umpire, others fill the scorebooks, others drink beer and shout from the stands. Kersi Meher-Homji has found a place of his own from which to observe a game that has fascinated him since childhood, a place between the players and the reporters which he has filled with determination and humour. He delves into the game with the delight of a child upon a Christmas stocking, and generally emerges with a point that the rest of us had missed. He is a cricketing man blessed with a logical and meticulous mind that finds satisfaction in the peculiar mixture of beauty, violence and mathematics that sets cricket apart.

Much can be told from Kersi's annual appearance at the Test match in Sydney. Of course he arrives modestly, almost sheepishly, though he is a familiar and respected figure whose warmth is widely appreciated. He joins his fellow writers in the back room, discussing the game or else waiting upon the arrival of the samosas, the highlight of the day as far as most reporters are concerned. At such times he conveys patience to which a certain craftiness must be added as another delicacy appears upon his plate. Kersi is not a man to underestimate.

Throughout Kersi smiles and talks thoughtfully about the game, often producing a telling statistic from the depths of his memory. He understands journalists and this game of bat and ball. Discretion counts amongst his strong points. Kersi will not walk up to a journalist and say, 'What utter nonsense you wrote yesterday!' Rather he will ask after a fellow's offspring and congratulate him upon sundry pertinent observations before gently observing that some minor inaccuracy had crept into the copy, doubtless due to misbehaviour on

Peter Roebuck, always looking for new angles. *(K.M.-H.)*

the part of the laptop. Somehow Kersi remains unaffected by the noise around him and the vicissitudes of the game as he goes about his affairs in his own quiet way. He is a dove amidst hawks.

Sometimes, during those visits to the Sydney press box, Kersi mentions that he has written a book about some part of the game that has attracted his attention. Since he is not a man in thrall to fame and fortune, it usually emerges that he has written an esoteric contemplation requiring much diligent research. Whereas most writers go for boundaries, Kersi pushes his score along steadily, collecting ones and twos and never mind that the crowd does not notice, till, finally, he reaches three figures.

In this book Kersi tells the story of the men who have played 100 Test matches, and more particularly their performances in that 100th match. As ever, Kersi sets the scene, provides the facts and adds insights into the characters involved. His accounts of past and present players confirm the thoroughness of his research and the extent of his understanding of the game and life itself. He talks about the great men of the game, including Shane Warne, whose 100th Test was an epic in its own right, and Sachin Tendulkar, who was subdued in his 100th match, as if worn out by the expectations.

Cricket enthusiasts will enjoy the contents of this book, especially the recollections of the struggles involved. Although a mathematical feat is the common factor in this study, Kersi never forgets that cricket is a story about the humanity of the players, their mighty achievements and their numerous flaws. Every chapter is different because these centurions are men of varying faith, colour, confidence and background. He tells their stories with the kindliness and sensitivity that count amongst his own strong points, and which he forgets only when news breaks in the Sydney press box that the samosas are on their way.

Peter Roebuck
May 2003

Acknowledgments

It is my pleasure to thank Peter Roebuck, my favourite cricket writer, for his perceptive and humorous Foreword — all the way from the Caribbean, C. Keshava Murthy for his statistical assistance, Carl Harrison-Ford for editing my eighth book in ten years (a record?) and Tricia Ritchings for word-processing my seventh book in nine years (another record?).

My thanks also go to those 100-Test heroes who spared time for me either by giving live interviews, speaking to me on the telephone or corresponding via e-mail. I was fortunate to meet and chat with some of these centurions in the press box during the 2002–03 Ashes series. As luck would have it, 12 of the surviving 26 centurions were in Sydney in January 2003, and most of them found time to share their 100th Test experiences with me. My special thanks to David Boon, David Gower, Mark Taylor, Ian Healy, Graham Gooch, Mike Atherton and Alec Stewart. I am grateful to David Clarke, England's media manager, for organising a meeting with Alec Stewart. Sunil Gavaskar and Dilip Vengsarkar readily responded to my e-mails.

Although Geoff 'Henry' Lawson played only 46 Tests, he dismissed Geoff Boycott and Clive Lloyd in their 100th Tests. I rang Lawson frequently for his help and he rallied round with an 'anything for you, Kersi' quote. Thank you, Henry.

Peter Roebuck was another font of knowledge and I have quoted him frequently.

The State Reference Library of NSW in Sydney was a treasure trove where I went through newspapers of the last 35 years on microfiche to delve into most cricketers' 100th Tests.

When lost in the dark, I turned to my friends and cricket scribes from India, Rajesh Kumar, Gulu Ezekiel, Clayton Murzello, Khalid Ansari, Indra Vikram Singh and C. Keshava Murthy, and they sent me rare and yellowing press clippings. Rajesh Kumar also checked the statistics. My gratitude also to Dr Colin Clowes of the NSW Cricket Library and to my sister Villy for her constant encouragement.

Andy Ganteaume, the one-Test hero who scored 112 runs in his only Test innings for the West Indies in 1948, and his friend Mervyn 'Pee Wee' Wong also supplied nuggets of information. Merci beaucoup to my friends David and Scilla Rosenberg and all at Rosenberg Publishing for their confidence that one day I'll pen a bestseller.

For photographs, I thank Ruth Gray (Getty Images), *Sportstar* (India), Clayton Murzello (*Mid-Day*, India), GE Features, Ken Hill, Rowley Morris, Ronald Cardwell and Stamp Publicity.

The books and magazines consulted have been listed in the Bibliography. However, four publications have been my constant companions: *Wisden Cricketers' Almanack* (spanning three centuries), *Wisden Cricket Monthly* (spanning three editors, founder David Frith, Tim de Lisle and Stephen Fay) and two volumes of *The Wisden Book of Test Cricket* compiled by Bill Frindall.

Symbols and Abbreviations Used

*	= Not out
5w/i	= Five wickets in an innings
10w/T	= Ten wickets in a Test
ABC	= Australian Broadcasting Corporation
ACB	= Australian Cricket Board
Aus	= Australia
Ave.	= Average
Eng	= England
BCCI	= Board of Control for Cricket in India
ECB	= England and Wales Cricket Board
Cat.	= Catches
HS	= Highest score
ICC	= International Cricket Council
Ind	= India
LOI	= Limited-Overs International
MCC	= Marylebone Cricket Club

MCG = Melbourne Cricket Ground
NO = Not out
N.S.W. = New South Wales
N.Z. = New Zealand
Pak. = Pakistan
PCB = Pakistan Cricket Board
S.A. = South Africa
SCG = Sydney Cricket Ground
S.L. = Sri Lanka
St. = Stumped
WACA = Western Australia Cricket Association
W.I. = West Indies
Wkt = Wickets
WSC = World Series Cricket
Zim. = Zimbabwe

Name Changes

Cities in India where important matches were played have gone through name changes in the last few decades. To avoid confusion, they are as follows: Bombay to Mumbai; Calcutta to Kolkata; Madras to Chennai; Mysore to Karnataka. Also, in Australia, the Sheffield Shield is now named Pura Cup.

They called David Gower laid-back, but he was all grace and elegance.
(Stamp Publicity)

Dedicated in memory of my beloved brother Behram
who first instilled in me the love of cricket.
A caring physician, he gave generously of his life to one and all.

Introduction

The book is a smorgasbord of assorted characters. They include a Lord and a Master Blaster, a Gorilla and a Super Cat, a Sultan of spin and a pair of twins. There are record holders in batting, bowling, downing most cans of beer on a Sydney to London flight and chewing most gum in the first slip. Then there are the most prolific cricketers to the greediest, the most graceful to the most belligerent.

Such many splendoured characters colour the book. The common link between them is that each one of them has played at least 100 Test matches, from Lord Cowdrey in 1968 to Carl Hooper in 2003.

In the Cape Town Test against South Africa on 8 March 2002, Shane Warne became the 25th cricketer, seventh Australian, fifth bowler and first spinner to play 100 Tests. It was a memorable Test for him. He scored 63 runs off 65 balls (hitting 10 fours and a six) adding 132 runs with Adam Gilchrist, and an unbeaten 15, captured eight wickets off 98 overs (including a winning spell of 70-15-161-6 in the second innings). He also took a catch and was at the non-striker's end when Australia won by four wickets to wrap up the Test series and the World Championship of Test cricket.

During this Test he also became the fourth cricketer after New Zealander Richard Hadlee, India's Kapil Dev and Pakistan's Wasim Akram to reach the Test double of 2000 runs and 400 wickets. Warne's role in Australia's win was vital because in the second innings South Africa appeared in a commanding position at 2 for 254, but his dismissal of Graeme Smith for 68 and Jacques Kallis for 73 tilted the game the visitors' way. Also when he came in to bat, Australia were 6 for 305, still needing 26 to win. Nonchalantly, he scored more than half of that target and was the worthy Man of the Match.

This may not be the greatest 100th Test ever but is certainly the inspiration behind the book. Six other cricketers had outstanding 100th Tests, seven had satisfactory ones and the remaining 13 had nothing to celebrate but the occasion. Now to those cricketers, referred in the book as 'centurions,' who did exceptionally well in their 100th Tests (in chronological order):

England's great batsman Colin Cowdrey was the pioneering member of the Centurion Club. He marked the occasion by scoring 104 runs against Australia in Birmingham in July 1968 and reaching 7000 runs in Test annals.

India's Kapil Dev shone out as an all-rounder. Against Pakistan in Karachi in November 1989, he scored 55 runs and took 4 for 69 and 3 for 82, capturing his 350th Test scalp. In that series 15 days later, the controversial Javed Miandad made 145 in Lahore. In April 1990, West Indian opener Gordon Greenidge hit 149 against England at Antigua, the highest score recorded by a player in his 100th Test. He emulated Miandad by scoring a century in both his first and 100th Tests and Cowdrey by reaching 7000 runs in this match.

Steve Waugh made 85 (adding 116 runs with brother Mark) in the SCG Test against South Africa in January 1998. Alec Stewart scored 105 for England against the West Indies at Manchester in August 2000, coincidentally on Queen Mother's 100th birthday. This remains the only Test in which two players played their 100th Tests together, the other being Stewart's team-mate Mike Atherton who could manage only one and 28 runs. Warne made his 100th Test memorable by becoming the only centurion to take five wickets in an innings.

Seven players performed reasonably well in their 100th Tests: England's Geoff Boycott (17 and 60), India's Sunil Gavaskar (48 and 37 runs and three catches) and Sachin Tendulkar (54), West Indians Viv Richards (68 runs and two catches including his 100th catch and leading his country to a victory against Australia), Desmond Haynes (18 and 57 not out) and Courtney Walsh (2-47 and 3-25), and Australian elegant icon Mark Waugh (32 and four catches).

The remaining 13 had disappointing 100th Tests. Perhaps the most forgettable was by Allan Border against the mighty Windies on the MCG in 1988. The first Australian to play 100 Tests, he arrived on the crease on Boxing Day amid thunderous applause. Five balls later he was back in the pavilion, bowled by Curtly Ambrose for a duck. The 26,287 dazed spectators could scarcely believe what they saw.

Test cricket was almost 92 years old when it produced the first centurion, Cowdrey. In the next 35 years, 26 have joined him, an indication of mushrooming of Test matches since the 1970s.

The centurions include 19 specialist batsmen, four all-rounders, two wicket-keeping batsmen and two specialist bowlers. Not bypassed are those who have played between 90 and 99 Tests. The most striking member of this group is India's Mohammad Azharuddin, who scored a century in his 99th and last Test. He was then discarded from any form of cricket because of his alleged involvement with illegal bookmakers. What a way to go!

More than just the statistics, the drama associated with each cricketer's 100th Test appearance is accentuated. The book attempts to detail the performances of all the 27 centurions in their 100th Test, and rated on a scale of 0 to 10. They have contributed richly to the game; as players, leaders, innovators and/or entertainers. They are the marathon runners of Test cricket; some of them were just as adept at 100 metre sprints.

Praying for a miracle? Shane Warne's 100th Test was perhaps the best of all.
(Ken Hill)

1 Colin Cowdrey

Colin Cowdrey was immaculate in everything he did. And modest. So modest that he did not realise how great a player he really was. Once Fred Trueman, his contemporary and the first to capture 300 Test wickets, described him as 'a terrific talent who never fulfilled his potential.'

Had he been ruthless and win-at-any-cost, he would not have been the Colin Cowdrey we loved and admired. He resembled a cuddly teddy bear with chubby cheeks. He was a kindly uncle you did not have; never an unpleasant word from him for friend or opponent. A unique and engaging personality, he will be remembered as much for his glorious cover drives as for his pudgy smile and humility.

He was destined to be a cricketer; his cricket-crazy father, Ernest — a tea planter — saw to it. He christened him Michael Colin Cowdrey — MCC for short — and taught him how to play with a straight bat at the age of four on a tennis court in Ootacamund, in the south of India, his birthplace. Even at that age, leg-side slogging was prohibited. 'Gradually my education widened and by the time I was 12, I could play most of the shots,' he recalled in *MCC: The Autobiography of a Cricketer.* Born on 24 December 1932, boy Cowdrey grew up to become one of the greats of the game, scoring 7624 runs at 44.07 in 114 Tests with 22 centuries and taking 120 catches. Both his run aggregate and catches accepted were then Test records. More important for this book, he was the first cricketer to play 100 Tests.

His 100th Test was played at Edgbaston, Birmingham, in July 1968 against his favourite foes, Australia. And what a match to savour for the gentle giant! It was the third Test in the series and England was trailing 0-1. It started on 12 July after the first day was washed out. Captaining his country, Cowdrey, 35, won the toss and batted. The English openers John Edrich and Geoff Boycott (36) had put on 80 runs when Cowdrey went in to bat.

He added 108 runs with Edrich before there was a mini collapse when Australian medium pacer Eric Freeman dismissed Edrich for 88 and the reliable Ken Barrington for a duck. From 1 for 188, England had plummeted to 3 for 189. To make matters worse, Cowdrey pulled a muscle in his left leg and used Geoff Boycott as a runner. He was on 58 then and two runs later became only the second player after another English great, Wally Hammond, to score 7000 runs in Test cricket. He was obviously in pain, but in true English bulldog spirit he carried on gamely with a stiff upper lip to match his stiff lower limb.

It was tough going, the left thigh hurting more as the day progressed. A crowd of about 20,000 saw history in the making the following morning. By now the approaching milestone of the English captain reaching his 100 in his 100th Test was anticipated by most of the spectators. 'He remained on 99 for 19 deliveries, the century obviously a landmark of great importance to the man personally,' wrote Phil Wilkins in *the Sydney Morning Herald.*

At last after half an hour of caution, he gained the single all had been waiting for; a defensive push off Graham McKenzie behind point to touch an unscaled peak. He was cheered to the echo and 'few men who had scored five runs in half an hour can claim that honour,' remembers Wilkins. Cowdrey had taken 235 minutes to reach this milestone. He remained only nine more minutes. Celebrating his 24th birthday, Freeman (4 for 78 in 30.5 overs) forced the rotund centurion to play the ball on to his wicket with a delivery a fraction off the off stump.

There were some magnificent strokes among Cowdrey's 15 boundaries, the cover drive especially being memorable because of the disdainful ease with which he played it. He had added 93 runs with another touch specialist, Tom Graveney, who went on to score 96. But the morning had belonged to the most charming of men, Colin Cowdrey. This was his 21st Test ton and surprisingly his first and only one against Australia in England.

Although advised rest for one week, Cowdrey fielded during the brief interval before tea. Then Graveney took over as the captain. Coincidentally, Australian captain Bill Lawry also retired hurt when

Colin Cowdrey will be remembered as much for his glorious cover drives as for his humility. *(Getty Images)*

his right-hand little finger was fractured in fast bowler John Snow's opening over. McKenzie deputised as captain when Australia fielded again. It was a rare instance of both Test teams being skippered by deputies.

To England's 409, Australia replied with 222, Ian Chappell top-scoring with 71. England declared at 3 for 142 to set Australia a winning target of 330. But rain ended the match at noon on the final day when Australia was 1 for 68 and needed 262 runs to win in 270 minutes. It was a damp ending to a match which had provided at least one magic moment.

Cowdrey missed the next Test at Headingley, Leeds, but returned to captain England in the final Test at The Oval. Although his scores were only 16 and 35, he had the satisfaction of leading England to a

226 run victory with only five minutes to spare and tied the Ashes series one-all. There was an incredible finish. A freak storm completely flooded the playing area on the final day but the sun's appearance and dedicated ground staff and volunteers enabled match to resume at 4.45 p.m.

Needing 352 runs to win, Australia was struggling at 5 for 86 then. However, opening bat John Inverarity dug in and appeared to have saved the match when, at 5.24 p.m., Cowdrey brought spinner Derek Underwood back in the attack. This sent the Aussies packing, Ashley Mallett and McKenzie fell to his first and sixth balls for ducks. In a breath-taking final five minutes, Inverarity (defending for 250 minutes for 56) padded up to an Underwood delivery and was adjudged lbw. England won because of Underwood's deadly spell of 7 for 50 and Cowdrey's, for once, inspiring leadership.

Cowdrey's one big ambition was to lead his country in Australia, and with this Ashes-leveling performance he seemed more firmly in the saddle than ever before for the 1970–71 tour. Unfortunately, an Achilles tendon snapped at the wrong time and Ray Illingworth, a rank outsider, got the job. Cowdrey, then 38, was disappointed but kept smiling genially. He did not get another chance. In all he led England 27 times, winning eight of these and losing four. The unanimous judgment about his leadership was that he was indecisive, a captain incapable of inspiring his players. His contemporaries had different viewpoints. Fred Titmus summed him up as 'amazing talent, done without showing off.' Trevor Bailey opined that Cowdrey was too nice to demolish an attack truly and that he worried too much.

He did captain his county Kent with authority and brought in useful changes when elected President of MCC in the bicentenary year. He was knighted in 1992 and became a life peer in 1997, the first Englishman and second cricketer, after West Indian Learie Constantine, to be elevated to the House of Lords. Thus Colin Cowdrey became Sir Colin and then Lord Cowdrey, Baron Cowdrey of Tonbridge.

The cricket world mourned his death on 4 December 2000, aged 67, after suffering a stroke earlier in the year. Kind and thoughtful, he loved to be loved and was loved. Becoming the first man to play 100 Tests and to score a century in it was the stuff dreams are made of.

Rating for 100th Test: 7.5/10.

2 Geoff Boycott

The performing flea of English cricket, Geoff Boycott was a superb technician. He had strokes for every occasion but used them sparingly. If Colin Cowdrey was gregarious, Boycott was a loner. If Cowdrey did not know how good he was, Boycott certainly did. Had he wished, Boycott would have been an entertainer — he was that gifted — but he chose to be dour, removing any risk. He was a prolific run-gatherer, ever so mindful of his average. He tended to bore the onlookers and exasperate the selectors, who once dropped him after he scored 246 dreary runs in a Test match. Unlike contemporary greats Viv Richards and Ian Botham, he worried more where his feet were when executing a shot rather than where the ball he stroked had gone.

Born on 21 October 1940 in Yorkshire, Boycott was the runner for an injured Cowdrey when the latter scored the last 46 runs of his 104 in his 100th Test in 1968. Even then, when Boycott had played 35 Tests, he would have fantasised about such a milestone for himself.

That day dawned 13 years later almost to the day. It was also against Australia in England. It was on Lord's, no less, in the second Test of the series with Australia leading 1-0. Will he do a Colin Cowdrey? The statisticians rubbed their hands in anticipation while the spectators had a resigned look. When Boycott wants a hundred that badly, he usually gets it even if it takes days.

Australian captain Kim Hughes won the toss and sent England in to bat. Boycott was the first to fall, caught Terry Alderman bowled Geoff Lawson for 17. A bit of an anticlimax, but the first two days had belonged to quickie Lawson who bowled superbly to capture 7 for 81 as England made 311.

Lawson vividly remembers this Test after 22 years. 'The Lord's Test was constantly rain-interrupted. We were on and off the field and I think I had 12 spells to complete my 43 overs. Geoffrey [Boycott] looked very confident to make a big score and I was pleased to get him out. I bowled an inswinger, he nicked it, it bounced off AB's [Allan Border's] hand from second slip and was caught by Terry Alderman in the first slip. Boy, was he disappointed. And he showed it!'

Not to worry, there was still the second innings for Boycott to emulate Cowdrey. Australia gained a narrow 34 run lead and Boycott was back at the crease, determination written all over him. England began the final day with Boycott still unbeaten and just three runs short of his 14th half-century in Tests against Australia. This was achieved and he added 123 runs with the stylish David Gower (89) for the third wicket. This steered England out of the harm's way but it remained to be seen whether the dour Yorkshireman could reach a century to match the occasion. His dream, however, fell 40 runs short of being realised. After four hours and 40 minutes of patient grinding, he reached for a Dennis Lillee delivery and was on his way to the pavilion when rubbery wicket-keeper Rod Marsh took a diving catch. Boycott appeared crushed. The Test was drawn and a rudderless England still trailed 0-1.

Apart from missing out on a century in his Test centenary, his bigger disappointment was not being asked to captain England in this and subsequent Test series. According to noted cricket writer Ian Wooldridge after that Test, 'On grounds of experience, mental hardness, strategic perception, self-discipline and the fact that he is the best of only three world-class players in the England side, he is the only man remotely equipped to whip rather than cajole England out of their present slump.' To make matters worse he was also rejected as vice-captain and was thus not even in the running. A dejected Boycott once said, 'Even the Yorkshire ripper got a fair trial in the dock but I've not been given a single chance.' (Earlier, he had captained England four times and had won one and lost one Test.)

Like his favourite sports stars Jack Nicklaus and Bjorn Borg, he avoided even mild social commitment when there was a major job ahead. 'Boycott, in short, walks alone,' added Wooldridge. This was what went against his claims to lead his country; he was more of an individual than a team-binder (or is it bonder?). But then Sir Donald

A classical cover-drive from Geoff Boycott. *(Stamp Publicity)*

Bradman was also a loner and his captaincy record was quite impressive, winning 15 out of the 24 Tests he skippered.

Boycott's 100th Test was Botham's last as captain. Botham made a pair in this Test and was replaced by Mike Brearley at the helm. And what a transformation for England! They incredibly won the next Test at Leeds after following on 227 runs behind and being 7 for 135 in the second innings. It was Botham's Test, his unbeaten 149 in the second knock converted a certain defeat into a sensational 18 run win. England went on to win the series comfortably, which made Brearley's position as captain secure and snuffed out any captaincy ambition for Boycott.

After retirement from cricket he became a cricket commentator and impressed with his knowledge and tactical acumen although his strong Yorkshire accent at times irritated listeners. Described as a selfish cricketer by his critics, his philosophy was that every run scored by him helped his team, be it his club, Yorkshire or England. Not many know that he readily advised team-mates and opponents on technical aspects of batting.

My lasting memory is of Boycott offering valuable tips to Pakistan's wonder boy Javed Miandad, then aged 19 in the visitors' dressing room during the 1976–77 Sydney Test. The teenager had just returned to the pavilion after scoring 64 splendid runs on a lightning-fast SCG strip against Lillee at his demonic best. I don't know what Boycott was doing in the Pakistani dressing room but I saw him, in a singlet and shorts, demonstrating to Miandad the correct way to cover drive. 'If you drive like what you did today, you'll get caught in the "goolly" [gully] in England.' But Miandad, arrogant even then, brushed aside this help and looked the other way. After a gutsy 64 against Lillee, Max Walker and Gary Gilmour, he thought he did not need private tuition.

The point of the story is that Boycott was not as selfish as he was often portrayed. Single-minded, certainly, obsessed with success, yes. However, his strong points were ignored and his self-centred, introverted side exaggerated. Controversial, outspoken and at times cantankerous, he was a classical batsman who loved the game. In 108 Tests he scored 8114 runs at 47.73, compiling 22 centuries with an unbeaten 246 as his highest. He never got married. He was married to cricket.

Rating for 100th Test: 4/10.

3 Clive Lloyd

Alec Bannerman, a Test cricketer of 1880 vintage and later a cricket coach, often told his trainees: 'Son, if you are not a cricketer, you can at least look like one.' If a prototype Test cricketer was to be created, Geoff Boycott would get my vote; cap tilted at the correct angle, well-creased white shirt and pants, a bat in hand as if an extension of his personality. Even in his shorts and singlet when he gave unsolicited advice to Javed Miandad in the SCG dressing room he appeared a complete cricketer.

The same cannot be said for Clive Hubert Lloyd, a far more attractive batsman and fielder and one of the greatest captains in the history of the game. Awkward, stooping, horn-rimmed spectacles on his nose, he appeared more like a University Professor, an accountant or a soul singer to non-cricket devotees. Even when he came out to bat in his cricket flannels, the uninitiated might have wondered whether he would reach the middle without tripping himself — let alone face Jeff Thomson on a green WACA pitch or B.S. Chandrasekhar on a Chepauk turner. Do not, however, waste your sympathy on the batsman; save it for the bowlers.

Watch out for the sudden transformation. You will imagine a telephone booth appearing from nowhere where 'Clark Kent' Lloyd would discard his glasses and don the Superman outfit as he took guard. As he is nicknamed Super Cat, this is not entirely your imagination. And paradoxical it may sound, there is something classical about his batting. A straight bat for good length deliveries on the front foot and a delicate glance or a cut to get off the mark would indicate that the left-handed batsman is settling in, a frightful thought for the bowler, but gave an inkling of excitement for the onlookers.

Clive Lloyd playing the innings of his life, a masterly century in the Prudential World Cup final at Lord's in June 1975. *(Gift from Ronald Cardwell)*

Just then the bowler tries a bouncer and the soul singer turns into a ballerina. Twinkle-toed, he would pull the offending hapless quickie for another four.

A similar kaleidoscopic transformation was visible when Clive Lloyd fielded in slips or covers, looking like an absent-minded professor on the verge of a discovery. Is he asleep, the ignoramuses among the audience might wonder. If so, they were in for a rude shock. He would propel his hand from nowhere to catch the flier or stop a sizzling cover drive, pick it up and flick it back to the bowler or 'keeper in one fell swoop to run out a complacent batsman. This achieved, he appeared to go back to his reverie, probably on some intricate scientific discovery.

He was born on 31 August 1944 in Georgetown, the second child and first son of Arthur and Sylvia Lloyd, a middle-class family in Guyana. Arthur was a chauffer for a local doctor and Sylvia looked after the increasing family with love and care. Inspiration to indulge in serious cricket came from his first cousin, Lance Gibbs — ten years his senior and a world-class off-spinner (who took 309 wickets at 29.09 in 79 Tests, becoming the second bowler after England's Fred Trueman to capture 300 Tests scalps). Although his cousin's success was a spur, it was self-motivation which carried him from school, club and first-class cricket to international renown: 'all the time, there was the goal of being a Test cricketer,' Lloyd wrote in *Living for Cricket*, his autobiography.

What is the genesis of his wearing glasses? He explains: The incident which caused another addition to the four-eyed variety of the human race occurred when he was 12 years old. 'Walking home from school, I noticed two younger boys engaged in a furious fight. Always the mediator, I stepped in to part them and got a knock in the right eye with a ruler for my troubles.' It was painful but young Clive ignored it till his vision deteriorated and he found it difficult to read the blackboard in school and scoreboard on the field. So he visited an optician who recommended spectacles becoming — for better or worse — part of the Lloyd image for evermore.

His first-class debut for Guyana against star-studded Barbados (including Charlie Griffith and Garry Sobers) was dramatic. He made a duck in the first innings which made Sobers comment to Berkeley Gaskin, a former fast-medium bowler for the West Indies and father figure for Clive, 'I see your boy didn't get any.' Berkeley responded in a flash: 'It's not my boy but a boy I like — and don't forget there is a second innings.' Clive overheard this and resolved not to let Berkeley — or himself — down in the second knock. 'This is the effect any criticism has had on me as long as I've held a cricket bat,' he reveals in *Living for Cricket.* With Guyana on its knees, trailing by 300 odd runs, Lloyd came in at 4 for 86 and scored a scintillating 107.

To show this was not a flash in the pan, he scored 194 against Jamaica at Sabina Park in Kingston. He had arrived and was a certainty for the tour to England in 1966 but was not picked. It was heart-wrenching for the 21-year-old Clive. 'To say that I was dumbfounded would be to put it mildly,' he remembers. 'I am not ashamed to say that I cried the night the news came through.' Lance Gibbs tried to console him but the tears kept rolling.

However, his international entry was delayed by only a few months. I was fortunate to be present when Lloyd made his Test debut at the Brabourne Stadium in Bombay (now Mumbai) in December 1966. The unpredictable leg-spinner Chandrasekhar bowled magnificently to claim 7 for 157 in the first innings and 4 for 78 in the second; his match figures of 11 for 235 were then a record for any Test in Mumbai. However, debutant Lloyd played him confidently, scoring 82 in the first innings and an unbeaten 78 in the second. He added 110 runs with Conrad Hunte for the fourth wicket and 50 with skipper Sobers for the fifth. In the second innings, he was once again associated in an unbroken 102 run stand with Sobers and the Windies won by six wickets.

To quote Lloyd from *Living for Cricket*: 'We had heard a lot about Chandrasekhar and the slight impediment of his right arm, which gives him a freakish action and makes the ball fizz off the pitch … It took some time for me to work him out for he really did mix things up. I began shakily and was put down early on at slip off his bowling, but after a while I decided to treat him purely as a googly bowler.'

I was equally privileged to watch Lloyd's final Test innings, an effervescent 72 in the Sydney Test of 1984–85, his 110th. Only Colin Cowdrey had then appeared in more Test matches, 114. Captain Lloyd made 33 and a top score of 72 — adding 60 runs for the fifth wicket with Viv Richards. It was a significant passing of the baton, from Sobers in his first Test to Richards in his last.

Unfortunately, Lloyd went out on a losing note although his team had retained the Frank Worrell Trophy by crushing Australia in the first three Tests. He received a hero's farewell from the Sydney crowd. He had scored 7515 runs at 46.68 in 110 Tests, belting 19 centuries. He had led the team 74 times (a record since broken by Allan Border, 93 times), winning 36 and losing only 12 Tests. Under him, West Indies had grown to a state of near invincibility — drawing comparisons with Don Bradman's 1948 team.

Lloyd will be remembered as much for his exciting left-hand batting as for his inspiring leadership. When he retired two headlines caught the eye: 'Exit the Bear From the World's Stage' and 'A Giant Lopes off Into the Sunset.'

Now to his 100th Test at Kingston, Jamaica in April–May 1984. It was the fifth and final Test against Kim Hughes' Australians. The Windies had already retained the Frank Worrell Trophy by winning the previous Test at St John's, Antigua, by an innings. To honour Lloyd for his 100th Test appearance, representatives of every West Indies Test team since 1938 were among those who took part in a special tribute to him on 30 April 1984, the first day of the Test.

'A capacity crowd of 15,000 gave out a roar that would have done Wembley Stadium proud when West Indies chairman, Mr Alan Rae, called three cheers for the first West Indian and the third cricketer to play 100 Tests,' wrote Peter McFarline in *the Sydney Morning Herald*. The tall, stooping, bespectacled Guyanian was presented with a silver salver by Rae, who highlighted Lloyd's Test career since his playing debut in 1966 and captaincy debut in 1974. Both the Australian and West Indian teams as well as Clive's wife Waveney (who flew out from England for this historic match) lined up in front of the George Headley Stand during the tea interval for the presentation.

Lloyd won the toss, sent Australia in to bat and unleashed his speed trio of Malcolm Marshall, Joel Garner and Michael Holding. Already trailing 0-2 in the series, the visitors lost four wickets before reaching 100 and were dismissed before reaching 200 — Border top-scoring with 41 in Australia's unimpressive total of 199. After a solid start of 162 by Gordon Greenidge (127) and Desmond Haynes (60) the home team lost Richie Richardson (0) and Viv Richards (2) cheaply. The score was 3 for 174 when in came Lloyd, cheered lustily by the crowd. He had scored only five when he hooked quickie Rodney Hogg high and wide but was dropped by the usually reliable Tom Hogan. Fifteen runs later, the Super Cat was acrobatically caught by wicket-keeper Wayne Phillips as he attempted a backfoot drive off Geoff Lawson.

Lawson was delighted when informed that he had dismissed two batsmen — Boycott and Lloyd — in their 100th Tests. Lloyd was sure that he had not got a touch and for once looked angrily at umpire David Archer. 'The umpiring was disgraceful,' Lawson agreed. 'But always in favour of the home team.' The Windies were then 4 for 213 and were dismissed for 305, a lead of 106. John Maguire had taken 4 for 57.

As Aussie opener Steve Smith's finger had been fractured by a lifter from Garner in the first innings, he was unable to take any further part in the match. Border stood between Australia and another humiliating innings defeat by scoring an unbeaten 60. However, with Marshall capturing 5 for 51 (for a match haul of 8 for 88), Australia was dismissed for 160. Needing 55 to win, the home team reached the target without losing a wicket. Lloyd had no second chance to shine in his 100th Test. He had, however, contributed handsomely in the 3-0 series win which was then their largest margin of victory in a rubber against Australia.

Triviologists pointed out that the Windies had not lost a wicket in the second innings in the entire series; 0 for 250 in the first Test in Guyana, 0 for 21 in the third Test in Barbados and 0 for 55 in the fifth and final Test in Jamaica. They had not batted in the second innings in the second and fourth Tests in Trinidad and Antigua.

By a coincidence, Lloyd's 100th Test was the 100th Test to be played in the Caribbean, West Indies winning 33, losing 18 and drawing 49. At the end of this historic Test, Lloyd presented rival captain Kim Hughes his jacket. Hughes reciprocated the gesture by presenting his jacket and cap to Lloyd during the post-Test dinner.

Lloyd, the master batsman and superb motivator, played many memorable innings. My favourite was his 102 in the inaugural World Cup final against Australia at Lord's in 1975. Against fierce opposition he scored an electrifying 102 while the normally exuberant Rohan Kanhai just gave support from the other end and applauded. Lloyd himself calls it 'one of the most enjoyable knocks I can remember playing.'

To quote the great fast bowler Wes Hall from *Living for Cricket*: 'Who can forget a sizzling Lloyd drive through mid-off or pull over mid-wicket? Who can forget the many great innings he has played for Guyana, his adopted Lancashire and the West Indies? Who can forget his century in the first World Cup Final? Who can forget his cat-like figure pouncing on the ball at cover and firing it with pinpoint accuracy back to the stumps for another run out? Who can forget a fielder I class along Colin Bland and Paul Sheahan as the best in my time?'

Apart from his magnificent batting and fielding, Clive Lloyd will be remembered for his leadership. Like Frank Worrell before him, he developed his players, built team spirit and made his team the strongest in the world. According to Lloyd, 'My greatest personal satisfaction has been that I have managed to achieve what I set out to do when appointed captain. This was to ensure that the West Indies team became a truly professional unit, each man aware of his responsibilities, dedicated to the cause of winning and believing in our collective ability.'

Richie Benaud, himself a great leader of men, said, 'West Indies have had two great captains — Frank Worrell and Clive Lloyd. Like Worrell, Lloyd is a father figure to his team and that is exactly what they need.'

Oh for a Worrell or a Lloyd to fix the Windies blues at the start of the new millennium!

Rating for 100th Test: 2.5/10.

4 Sunil Gavaskar

Mini-Atlas 'Sunny' Gavaskar carried India on his slender but determined shoulders. He was the best opening batsman of his time and one of the greatest openers of all time, staking comparisons with Jack Hobbs and Len Hutton, Bill Ponsford and Arthur Morris. Barely 165 cm tall, he faced the most ferocious fast bowlers in Test history without a helmet. Also without flinching! A failure by Gavaskar often precipitated an Indian batting debacle. Just have a look at the new-ball attack he had to encounter all his career, and for a country very much dependent on him to give a solid start.

The West Indies had Andy Roberts, Michael Holding, Malcolm Marshall, Joel Garner and Colin Croft; Australia had Dennis Lillee, Jeff Thomson, Lennie Pascoe, Rodney Hogg and Terry Alderman; England had John Snow and Bob Willis; Pakistan had Imran Khan, Sarfraz Nawaz and Wasim Akram; New Zealand had Richard Hadlee. And then there were the spinners ... Lance Gibbs, Derek Underwood and Abdul Qadir.

Sunil 'Sunny' Gavaskar took them head-on (pun not intended) and became the first batsman to top 10,000 runs (only Allan Border and Steve Waugh have exceeded his Test aggregate of 10,122 runs), the first one to score 30 Test centuries (his 34 tons is still a record, with fellow Mumbai maestro Sachin Tendulkar hot on his trail) and the only one to aggregate over 700 runs in his initial Test series, 774 runs at a Bradman-like average of 154.80 in four Tests, including a century and double century in one Test in the Caribbean in 1971.

He handled pace and spin masterfully and was twinkle-toed against spinners — from his first series to his last in 1987, giving a supreme exhibition of temperament and technique and scoring 96 in his final

Gavaskar hungry for runs. *(K.M.-H.)*

Test innings (at Bangalore against Pakistan). What a swan song! The next highest contributor was extras with 27 as India lost by just 16 runs. During this innings he completed 2000 runs against Pakistan and ended a Test career lasting 16 glorious summers holding the following world Test records: most Tests (125), most consecutive Tests (106), most innings (214), most runs (10,122), most centuries (34), most 50s (45) and most century partnerships (58). Most of these records have been eclipsed.

He was more than just a run-machine or a record-wrecker. He was an artist who chiselled out an innings; he played within his strengths, handled situations adroitly and was there when needed. His powers of concentration were such that he rarely gave his wicket away. Only two contemporary opening batsmen can be ranked with him, Geoff Boycott and Gordon Greenidge. However, Boycott for all his technical expertise tended to pick and choose his opponents. Greenidge was privileged that he did not have to face the 'chin music' from his fellow West Indian super-speedsters. In fact in 1978, West Indies great Sir Garry Sobers ranked Gavaskar as the greatest opening batsman in the post-1960 era.

It is not so surprising that Gavaskar played 125 Tests as that he played cricket at all. Born into a cricketing family, he grew up admiring his uncle Madhav Mantri's Test cap and blazer. (Mantri had played four Tests for India in 1950s as a wicket-keeper, taking eight catches and stumping one.) However, Sunil owes his success to another uncle, Narayan Masurekar, and a hole in his ear. Let Sunil tell this tale — abstracted from his autobiography, *Sunny Days*.

'I may never have become a cricketer if an eagle-eyed relation Narayan Masurekar had not come into my life the day I was born (on 10 July 1949). He had noticed a little hole near the top of my left ear lobe. When he came the next day he found to his horror that the baby did not have the hole on the ear. A frantic search of all the cribs in the hospital revealed that I was sleeping blissfully beside a fisherwoman. The mix-up followed after the babies were given their bath.'

The possibilities, the might-have-beens, are staggering. Would the fisherman's son in Sunil's nappy have turned out to be a cricketer, given that Sunil's father Manohar was a cricket fan and a better than average club cricketer, while Uncle Mantri would have coached and inspired that boy? More interesting: would the real Sunil have had the opportunity to hold a bat, let alone score over 10,000 Test runs, had he grown up in a fishing village with a cricket field miles away?

The babies sorted out, it was a rapid climb for Sunil Gavaskar; he went from backyard cricket to school, inter-school and inter-university cricket to Ranji Trophy and to Test fame with the same solid footwork that made him one of the most prolific run-getters of the century. He says he learnt to read numbers from scoreboards. While children his age went to sleep listening to stories of Red Riding Hood and Robin Hood, the three-year-old listened to John Arlott and Rex Alston commentating the 1952 Test series in England where uncle Madhav was wicket-keeping. 'For him the big bad wolf was Fred Trueman,' to quote cricket writer Dicky Rutnagur.

Gavaskar started his Test career in the grandest possible manner. Selected to tour the West Indies in 1971, the 21-year-old started off with 65 and 67 not out in Trinidad as India gained their first victory over West Indies at their 25th attempt. This was just a preview. In the following Test in Guyana he made 116 and 64 not out, followed by 1 and an unbeaten 117 in Barbados, and climaxed by stroking 124 and 220 in Trinidad. He had become only the second player after Doug Walters to hit a century and a double century in the same Test. More remarkable was the fact that he had achieved this despite an excruciating toothache and was refused painkillers by the tour manager in case they would make him drowsy. He could hardly sleep those four nights. 'Surprisingly, however, the pain sharpened my other instincts,' Sunil remembers. 'My reflexes were quicker and my concentration became more intense as the pain increased.'

This was perhaps Sunil's finest hour, as his run marathon enabled India to draw the Test and win the series 1-0. His prolific runmaking enabled Lord Relator to compose a calypso:

It was Gavaskar the master, just like a wall.
We couldn't out Gavaskar at all, not at all.
You know the West Indies couldn't out Gavaskar at all.

Each of his 34 Test centuries was a masterpiece, many of them played during crisis. His best perhaps was his memorable 221 against England at The Oval in 1979. India needed a massive 438 runs to win in 498 minutes and started slowly but steadily, Gavaskar and Chetan Chauhan putting on 213 for the first wicket. Then Dilip Vengsarkar joined him and the two Mumbai men scored at a run a minute. The last 20 overs began at 1 for 328, as India needed 110 more runs to win and the English, like the Windies eight years previously, 'couldn't out Gavaskar at all.' He masterminded the show. India was going serenely towards a magnificent victory when Ian Botham intervened. He took three quick wickets, a catch and effected a run out. Gavaskar's memorable 221 lasted 489 minutes and he hit 21 fours, cover drives predominating. The match ended as an engrossing draw as India made 8 for 429, nine runs short of victory.

Gavaskar became the first Indian and the fourth cricketer to play 100 Tests. This was in the first Test against Pakistan at Lahore in October 1984. Pakistan batted first and scored freely to total 428, Zaheer Abbas remaining unbeaten with a stroke-filled 168. Gavaskar accepted three catches which helped dismiss opening batsman Mudassar Nazar, wicket-keeper Ashraf Ali and off-spinner Tausif Ahmed.

Captaining India, Gavaskar top-scored with 48 as India collapsed for 156 to the swing of Azeem Hafeez who captured 6 for 46. This included Gavaskar's scalp. Forced to follow on, Gavaskar (37) and Anshuman Gaekwad (60) put on 85 for the first wicket. Then a fine unbeaten 101 by Mohinder Amarnath and 71 by Ravi Shastri enabled India to draw the Test. They added 126 runs for the fifth wicket, which saved India. Although not a crash hot Test for Gavaskar, it was not one to forget in a hurry. 'My recollection of my 100th Test was that of General Zia-ul-Haq, President of Pakistan, flying down from Islamabad to Lahore specially to congratulate and present me with a carpet on his behalf and a silver salver on behalf of the Lahore District Cricket Association for being the first from the subcontinent to play hundred Test matches,' Gavaskar told me recently. 'However, the Board of Control for Cricket in India did not present me with anything on that occasion.'

In 125 Tests, he had amassed 10,122 runs at 51.12, hitting 34 centuries (highest score an unbeaten 236 against the West Indies at Chennai in 1983–84) and took 108 catches. He had a pretty ordinary record as captain, winning only nine of the 47 Tests, losing eight and drawing 30. His greatest assets were his superb footwork and power of concentration that compensated his lack of centimetres.

There was another side of Gavaskar when he dug his heels in and refused to budge. For example, his leading a 'walk-out' in the February 1981 Melbourne Test when given out lbw to Dennis Lillee and boycotting the Kolkata Test of February 1987 to punish the crowd which had abused him in previous matches ... However, these were rare aberrations in an otherwise outstanding career. He was a role model with his courage, consistency and artistry. As a television commentator, he is articulate and perceptive. As a player Sunil Gavaskar received great praise from other cricketing greats:

Colin Cowdrey: 'He is quite simply a genius with a bat — one of the greatest attacking players of all time. I particularly remember watching him score 221 against England at The Oval in 1979, which was a fantastic display of batting.'

Fred Trueman: 'simply the best opening batsman in the world for many years ... But I'm afraid that he does not compare with Sir Len Hutton. He [Hutton] moved with the grace of a ballet dancer. However, Sunny is better than Geoff Boycott. Geoff had good defence but he is a one-pace player who lets the bowlers call the shots. Gavaskar had the ability to move into a higher gear whenever it suited him.'

Clive Lloyd: 'He was up against it throughout his career. I would not hesitate to put Sunny on the same pedestal as that of Sir Don. In fact, coming to think of it in the right perspective, Sunny deserves more credit.'

Don Bradman: 'He is a great player and an ornament to the game.'

Rating for 100th Test: 4/10.

5 David Gower

If batting was an Olympic event comparable to gymnastics, David Gower would have won many gold medals. An epitome of grace and elegance, he played with time to spare. One can say this of only few cricketers: Frank Woolley, Frank Worrell, Neil Harvey, Gundappa Viswanath, Graeme Pollock, Greg Chappell, Mohammad Azharuddin and Mark Waugh. A thirty from Gower provided more entertainment than a 130 from a mere mortal.

He appeared nerveless, unruffled and unflappable as he batted without inhibition. There were no big slogs from him, just superb timing. An imperious and exciting batsman, he made writers invent adjectives. Because of his blond and curly-topped hair and precocious brilliance, he was known in his early days as the Golden Boy of cricket. He began his Test career by hitting the first ball received for a four. This was against Pakistan at Edgbaston in June 1978. He went on to become the youngest to register a century for England since Peter May. According to noted English writer Christopher Martin-Jenkins, Gower 'was the most gifted cricketer to play for England since Denis Compton,' and added that his timing 'had the exquisite touch of Menuhin.' Even a hard to please man, Geoff Boycott, once told Gower, 'I wish I could bat like you.'

Born on the 1 April 1957, David Ivon Gower was no April fool, being a cerebral sportsman who studied law (although did not complete his degree — 'too boring'), enjoys classical music and solving crossword puzzles. He spent his early years in Tanganyika (as Tanzania was then called) in Africa where his father was in the Colonial Service. Although born in Tunbridge Wells and educated in Canterbury, he did not play for Kent. Leicestershire invited him first and thus started a long and successful but not permanent partnership with his county of adoption. Soon the golden boy scintillated in county cricket, one-day internationals and Test annals with his boundless natural talent, but he lacked consistency.

Like Mark Waugh, Gower was described as 'laid back' and 'taking things too lazily.' His cool confidence was at times mistaken for arrogance and a 'don't care' attitude. This is an allegation he does not entirely refute in his book,' *With Time to Spare* (co-authored by Alan Lee). He wrote: 'There ARE days when I feel lazy, when I know I have no adrenaline flowing and it is difficult to motivate myself.' He does, however, refute the claim that he is nerveless. He feels as tense as any player at the start of an innings, facing a team crisis or nearing a landmark. That 'cool cat' exterior occasionally cracked under pressure. Flashes of temper were rare for him but not unknown. Once when playing for Leicestershire against the touring Indians in 1979, he smashed down his stumps after playing a poor shot, but the anger was directed at himself. 'It was a way of releasing pent-up tension,' he said, but regretted such irrational and uncharacteristic behaviour.

He was also a magnificent outfielder who took amazing catches and threw with accuracy and power to run out a blasé batsman. Although he bats left-handed, he bowls and throws with his right arm, writes with his right hand, plays golf and hockey right-handed and kicks a football with his right foot. Perhaps he was inspired to bat left-handed watching his childhood heroes Graham Pollock and Garry Sobers. 'I tried to bat their way,' he remembers.

Edgbaston in Birmingham has been his favourite hunting ground. It was here that the 21-year-old made his Test debut scoring 58 (inclusive of a first-ball four off Liaqat Ali) against Pakistan as England won by an innings. It was also at Edgbaston that he made his highest Test score, an unbeaten 200 against India in July 1979 and 215 against Australia in August 1985.

The year 1985 was a golden season for him. In six Tests against Australia, he amassed 732 runs at 81.33 including 166 at Trent Bridge in Nottinghamshire, 215 at Edgbaston and 157 in the next Test at The Oval. He had the added satisfaction of leading England to a stunning 3-1 win, regaining the Ashes. He was engaged in big partnerships in the last two Tests; 331 runs with Tim Robinson (148) at Edgbaston and 351 runs with Graham Gooch (196) at The Oval, both for the third wicket.

The Gower innings I remember most vividly was in the Sydney Test of January 1991. He scored 123 runs in the first innings, but it was his shorter second innings which is etched in my memory. Set an impossible win target of 255 at 9.1 runs an over, the warhorses Gooch (54) and Gower (36) took up the challenge, adding 84 runs at seven runs an over for the first wicket before Gower was caught inside the long-off boundary after topping 8000 Test runs. When the two Gs were together, the impossible appeared almost possible. England lost the Test but it was heart-warming stuff.

Another memorable innings by Gower was his unbeaten match-saving knock of 154 against the West Indies in Kingston in April 1981. He earned England a draw by batting through the last 465 minutes, adding precious runs with Peter Willey and Paul Downton. By playing this sedate innings he proved Clive Lloyd wrong. Lloyd had described Gower as 'too self-centred.' Gower loved to prove fellow cricketers wrong.

On his ability to motivate, former England captain Bob Willis said, 'David was a good self-motivator, but I don't think he could motivate others.' Indeed there were times when Gower could not motivate himself, for example in his 100th Test at Headingley, Leeds, in July 1988.

It was a disappointing match for him, scoring only 13 and 2 runs and taking one catch (to dismiss top-scorer Roger Harper for 56). At 31, he was then the youngest to play 100 Tests by four years. He was the third English centurion, after Colin Cowdrey and Geoff Boycott, and there has been an interesting 'pass the baton' sequence. An injured Cowdrey had used Boycott as his runner during his century in his 100th Test. Boycott also added 123 runs with Gower (89) for the third wicket in his 100th. In Gower's 100th, the next English centurion Graham Gooch made 50. Also in this Test, Chris Cowdrey (son of Colin) captained England for the first time.

What are Gower's memories of his 100th Test? 'It was not a particularly special moment for me as my scores indicate,' Gower reminisced with me in the SCG press box during a December 2002 England–Australia one-dayer. 'This Test came at a time when I was not in great form and battling to keep my place in the side. The only pleasant memory of this Test for me was that Chris Cowdrey, a close friend of mine, was picked to captain England for the first time. Part of my job was to see young Chris through the match against the strong West Indians. As the visitors were in command throughout, it was a tough job to get him settled. I was happy to help and guide him.'

As far as Gower can remember, the English Cricket Board had not made any presentation to him to celebrate his milestone Test; no salver, no plaque. He recalled sadly that England lost this match by a big margin. Not surprisingly, he had forgotten that in this match he had done a Colin Cowdrey by reaching his 7000th Test run in his 100th Test. He was always a team man and cared little for personal landmarks.

He remembered vividly that it had rained a lot in this Test and that he was interviewed during one of the rain breaks by Brian Johnston for the *Test Match Special* television show. Recalled Gower, 'Throughout my career, Brian had called me "laid back" — my personality was laid back, my batting was laid back. Provocatively he asked me, "Are there any two words you would like to remove from the vocabulary?" He was sure I would say laid back but I took him by surprise by replying, "caught Dujon"!'

The unpredictable Gower was dropped in the next two Tests. This hurt him but he took it on the chin and went on to play 17 more Tests. He batted with time to spare and retired at the right time. Currently, he is involved in rhinoceros protection and organizes charity cricket matches for the Rhino Relief fund. Trust Gower to do something different, perhaps making rhinos laid-back!

'Gower's batting was the stuff of poetry and enriched the lives of those privileged to watch him,' wrote Martin Johnson in *Wisden 1994*. 'The proudest possession on his mantelpiece at home is a trophy from a national magazine. It is a plaque inscribed with the words, "For Fun, Style and Excellence" which was a perfect way of summing up his philosophy and career.'

Rating for 100th Test: 1/10.

6 Vivian Richards

Among all the 100 Test heroes adorning this book, Viv Richards and Sachin Tendulkar were the most spectacular. However, with India always struggling with an unreliable batting line-up (especially overseas) and a threadbare bowling attack, Tendulkar often had to curb his dazzling stroke-play. Not so Sir Vivian Richards. He had a fine array of batsmen to take over if he failed and the most menacing pace battery in cricket history. So he could indulge and indulge he did, putting extra rum in the Caribbean cola. He was both a master and a blaster, and was called 'Master Blaster.'

Only Don Bradman had a vaster crowd appeal. They called Bradman 'Don,' Tendulkar 'God' and Richards 'King.' In India Viv once did dress like a Maharajah in a shimmering robe and jewelled crown and looked the part. 'King' Richards resembled both a ballerina and a professional boxer with his graceful footwork and the knockout punches he threw. Hence his nickname — 'Smokin' Joe.'

Isaac Vivian Alexander Richards was born on 7 March 1952 in Antigua. It was clear from his school days that he had natural talent as a ball player. He represented Antigua in cricket and soccer as a teenager and was the idol of crowds. Paradoxically, it was his popularity that retarded his progress. Against St Kitts in 1969, Viv was wrongly given out caught for nought. His clear disapproval caused a riot, with his fans chanting 'No Viv, No Match.' Surprisingly, the match organizer recalled him. He was soon stumped without scoring a run. In the second innings he got another duck as he was caught in the cover. Thus, he had made three zeros in a match — an unenviable but unique feat. This, however, was not the worst fate to befall the 17-year-old. For showing dissent and thus sparking a riot, Viv was banned from playing cricket for two years.

'From being a golden boy, now I was in disgrace,' he wrote in *Sir Vivian: The Definitive Autobiography*.

There was an 'action replay' of this incident in the Jamaica Test against India in April–May 1989. Captaining his team, Viv had scored 110 runs off 178 balls, spanking 13 fours and a six. It was his 24th Test century (and as it turned out his last) when he was declared caught behind off Kapil Dev. When Viv showed his disappointment at the decision, there was a mini riot lasting 35 minutes. He was not banned this time. Who would dare punish the King!

These were rare aberrations in his otherwise sporting demeanour. It was Viv Richards' immense popularity from a teenager to a 37-year-old elder statesman that provoked crowd disturbance. His Test record was most impressive, despite his spirit of adventure and entertainment value. In 121 Tests, he scored 8540 runs at 50.24, blasting 24 centuries (highest score 291) and 45 fifties, took 32 wickets as an off-spinner at 61.38 and accepted 122 catches. His run aggregate, number of centuries, fifties and — for a non-wicket-keeper — catches were records for a West Indian. However, one cannot assess Viv by statistics alone; he was more than a run machine. Wrote *Wisden 1977*, 'Mere figures cannot convey his perfect style and stroke-play. His cover driving was superb, with his feet always in the right position and the way he flicked the ball on the leg stump to square leg had to be seen to be believed.'

Despite all his natural flair, boy Richards could not convert his potential to centuries. The youngster would get out when well set through a lack of concentration. This changed when he was sent to Alf Gover's Cricket School in London in 1973, financed by public subscription. He played county cricket for Somerset where the real Viv Richards stood up. Still he tended to throw away his wicket in the Caribbean and had not scored a first-class century there till 1974. Thus it was an inspired move by the West Indian selectors to pick him for the tour of India in 1974–75. He had trouble countering the spin of B.S. Chandrasekhar in his Test debut in Bangalore, failing in both innings. However, in the following Test in Delhi he was at his majestic best, pelting six sixes and 20 fours in his unbeaten 192. To use a cliché, a star was born. Each of Richards' centuries was a gem — as were some of his lower scores. At Test and limited-overs international levels (including World Cup), he was a supremo. His magnificent 138 not out (three sixes and 11 fours) in the 1979 Prudential World Cup final at Lord's is still remembered with awe.

It is impossible to nominate his best innings. My favourite is his double century in The Oval Test against England in August 1976. It was a glorious display, smacking 291 of the best with 34 fours in 472 minutes. In a high scoring match of many highlights, England totalled 435 (Dennis Amiss scoring a double century) and 203; Michael Holding capturing a record 14 scalps. But Viv was the hero as he passed Sir Frank Worrell's 261 which was the highest score by a West Indian in England and was behind the West Indies' 10 wicket victory. In four Tests he had amassed 829 runs at 118.42 (a record aggregate for one playing four Tests), with two masterpieces, 232 in the Trent Bridge Test and 291 at The Oval. In the calendar year 1976, he totalled 1710 runs — still a record — at 90.00.

Another masterpiece from Viv Richards came in the final Test in Antigua — his birthplace — against England in April 1986. In a sensational batting display, he slammed the fastest Test century in terms of balls received, 56. Leading 4-0 in the series, skipper Richards played a scintillating innings of 110 not out which included seven sixes (a total then exceeded only by Wally Hammond) and seven fours. It came off only 58 balls and 83 minutes. It was awesome. As the West Indies triumphed by 240 runs, they had 'blackwashed' England 5-0 for the second successive time.

The year 1988 in Australia was special for the Master Blaster as he scored his 100th first-class century and celebrated his 100th Test appearance by taking his 100th Test catch and scoring a dazzling 68. A week before his 100th Test, he recorded his century of centuries in a match against New South Wales on the SCG on 13 November. This was only the third instance that a cricketer had reached this milestone in Australia; the other two being E.H. 'Patsy' Hendren of England on the MCG in 1928–29 and Don Bradman against the touring Indians, on the SCG, in 1947–48. Viv was given a standing ovation by 6500 spectators when he completed his 100th first-class ton. 'This is something I will cherish for a long time and it is a wonderful feeling for me being the first West Indian to attain this landmark,' he said that night. (He remains the only West Indian to have achieves this feat.] His 101 included 15 fours and a monumental six before falling to Mike Whitney.

Viv's 100th Test started five days later, at the Gabba, Brisbane on 18 November. Would he repeat his SCG success of the previous week and become only the second player after Colin Cowdrey (that far) to record a century in his 100th Test, the press and public speculated.

'Raja' Richards bedecked with a turban and jewels. (*Sportsweek,* India)

On the opening day of the Test, Viv took his 100th catch. He ran 25 metres from slips towards long stop to make a superb interception to catch Tony Dodemaide off Courtney Walsh. This ended Australia's innings for 167 and was the first wicket in Walsh's unusual hat-trick which took an amazing 45 hours to complete. 'After much slapping of palms and patting of backs, he [Viv] led his conquering force from the ground, strong in the knowledge that they had reasserted their domination over Australia after just one day in the middle,' wrote Mike Coward in the *Sydney Morning Herald*. Viv had become the tenth fielder to accept 100 Test catches.

The next afternoon, skipper Viv went in to bat at 3 for 162 and played a dominating innings, adding 108 runs with Richie Richardson. Viv hit 11 fours and a six off Dodemaide in his exciting innings. Just when it seemed certain that he would reach his coveted ton, he fell 32 runs short. His 68 had come off only 78 balls in 109 minutes.

Remembers Phil Wilkins, 'Viv celebrated his 100th Test with a lavish display of fireworks. After Craig McDermott had worried him by bowling an off-cutter searing back over his stumps, then a bouncer which hissed near his eye-brows, Viv lashed out at off-spinner Tim May high to deep square leg. McDermott eyed it like a rare diamond and held the swirling catch.' Even the partisan Brisbane crowd was disappointed to see the Master Blaster's failure to reach a celebratory ton. This was a Test to remember for Viv as he led West Indies to a nine-wicket win with over a day to spare and eventually won the rubber 3-1.

Who can sum up Viv Richards flamboyant Test career better than his captain Clive Lloyd? He wrote in *Living for Cricket* (1980): 'In five years Vivian Richards has developed into a batsman who fully deserves the often misused title of "great." As his captain throughout that time, I have seen him mature from a player of raw natural talent, who was getting out just when he had settled in, into one with a thirst for big scores. Early on, he was nervous and tense before a big match and perhaps that accounted for the number of times he was dismissed between 20 and 60 but, with experience and the knowledge that everyone had faith in him, he became more certain of himself … He had a complete repertoire of strokes and with a build like a heavyweight boxer he gives the ball a tremendous whack. Brilliant in the field, capable of bowling off-spin and enthusiastic at all times, he has become a truly modern Superstar, the answer to any captain's dream.'

Viv Richards destroyed the most potent attack with crushing stroke-play and arrogant demeanour. He was a trendsetter and an improviser. Rather than be compared with others, later batsmen will be judged on his scale. He was unique.

Rating for 100th Test: 5/10.

7 Dilip Vengsarkar

Dilip Vengsarkar, the third highest run-scorer for India, was known as 'Colonel' — because he is tall and stately — and 'Master of Lord's' because he scored centuries in three consecutive Lord's Tests. He batted like a champion in England and India but struggled on the bouncy Australian and West Indian pitches. Fast bowlers did not worry him. However, horror movies scared him silly. He shut his eyes till the monster has disappeared from the screen. 'I respect Lillee, one of the best bowlers in the world, Rodney Hogg and Lennie Pascoe but I don't move away,' he told me in 1981. 'But horror movies scare me. I can't sleep for two to three nights after seeing one — even on television.' Rather unbecoming behaviour for a Master of Lord's and a Colonel!

In 116 Tests, Dilip Balwant Vengsarkar amassed 6868 runs at 42.13 with 17 centuries. Among Indians, only Sunil Gavaskar and Sachin Tendulkar have scored more runs and centuries. And among non-Englishmen, he holds the unique record of hitting hundreds on every one of his consecutive Test appearances at Lord's; 103 in 1979, 157 in 1982 and an unbeaten 126 in 1986. He reached his peak on the 1986 tour of England, topping the first-class match average scoring 536 at 67.00 and Test average for both sides, making 360 at 90.00 with hundreds at Lord's and Headingley, Leeds. This was the highest Test average by any Indian batsman in a Test series in England but has since then been eclipsed by Rahul Dravid, who averaged 100.33 in 2002. To make Dilip's joy complete, India won both these Tests and eventually won the series 2-0.

Vengsarkar had mainly engineered the Lord's victory in 1986. His unbeaten 126 came off 213 balls in 326 minutes and included 16 fours. His tenth Test ton was full of classical elegance and old world

Dilip 'Colonel' Vengsarkar (standing) with team-mates Ashok Malhotra and Mohinder Amarnath, and a young fan. *(K.M.-H.)*

charm; his off-side drives simply majestic. He was stranded on 81 when India lost her eighth wicket but the tailenders helped him reach his century and go beyond. He carried on in the same easy manner in the second innings when India was set a victory target of 134. India lost 2 for 31 but Vengsarkar top-scored with 33 and India won by five wickets.

He was the Man of the Match in the next Test in Headingley. On one of the poorest Test pitches seen in England in years, he once again top-scored for India with 61 and India took a commanding 170 run lead. However, they frittered away this advantage losing 4 for 35 and 5 for 70. Who should come to India's rescue but the Colonel, who struck 102 not out. India outplayed England by 279 runs in three and half days. He had totalled 322 runs in the first two Tests at a Bradmanesque average of 161.00.

Born on 6 April 1956 in Mumbai, Dilip made headlines as a 19-year-old by hammering seven sixes off master spinners Bishan Bedi and E.A.S. Prasanna on a turning pitch to make a chanceless 110 for Ranji Trophy champions (Mumbai) against Rest of India in 1975. This led to his being selected in an unofficial test against Sri Lanka in Hyderabad as an opening partner for Sunil Gavaskar. He made only 1 and 17 and was dropped. It was heart-breaking for a talented teenager, perhaps as bad as watching a Dracula movie. The next month, however, he hit back, belting an unbeaten 108 for Combined Universities against the Sri Lankans. A few months later he was on the plane to New Zealand where he made his Test debut and then to the West Indies. The Windies captain Clive Lloyd was impressed by Dilip's technique on a treacherous, bouncy Kingston strip and commented that it was 'the best innings played in a Test by a youngster.'

Vengsarkar's role models were Bob Simpson, Geoff Boycott and club mate Gavaskar. From them he learnt the art of building an innings. The result was five Test centuries against all cricket-playing countries in 1979. He attracted worldwide attention with his unbeaten 157 in the second innings of the Kolkata Test against the West Indies, adding 344 runs with Gavaskar for the unbroken second wicket. Was this his best innings? 'No, it has to be my 103 in the Lord's Test of 1979,' he replied. 'We started our second innings more than 300 runs in arrears. Yet we drew the Test as Viswanath and I added 210 runs. To be adjudged Man of the Match by John Arlott was a big moment for me.'

In the 1979 Bangalore Test against Australia, he hit Rodney Hogg for a couple of sixes in his 112. A year earlier in the run-rich Adelaide Test, he contributed 78 when India was challenged to make 493 for victory and scored 445. 'Imagine, totalling over 440 runs in the fourth innings and yet end up losing!' he lamented. Keith Miller described his upright batting stance as a model for youngsters.

Vengsarkar's 100th Test was against New Zealand in Mumbai in November 1988. Captaining India, he scored 25 and 0; caught by Tony Blain off John Bracewell in the first innings and bowled by Bracewell in the second. He accepted two catches, Richard Hadlee off Naren Hirwani for one and Ian Smith off Arshad Ayub for 54. As India lost the Test by 136 runs as well, it would be a Test to forget for the 'Colonel' I thought. On the contrary, he recalls it fondly. 'I still vividly remember the morning of my 100th Test on my home turf,' he said. 'Not many are so lucky, for at the time I was the captain of the team as well. We had won the first Test at Bangalore where I had scored 75 runs on a wicket that helped spinners from day one. I remember Richard Hadlee getting his 374th Test match wicket to break Ian Botham's record as I went out to face him. Coming back to my 100th Test, I received many telephone calls on the eve of the match and on the morning of the match. I also received a Fiat car from a wellwisher as a gift. Apart from that I did not receive any memento either from BCCI [Board of Control for Cricket in India] or from the Mumbai Cricket Association — which incidentally celebrated Sachin Tendulkar's 101st Test match at the Wankhede Stadium, Mumbai, in October 2002. We went to Hyderabad for the decider and won by ten wickets to win the rubber 2-1. Playing in one's 100th Test was a very satisfying feeling and a proud moment as well.'

Rating for 100th Test: 1.5/10.

8 Allan Border

Allan Border holds many Test records. He played the most Tests in a row (153), scored most runs (11,174) and captained his country in most Tests (an unbroken run of 93, winning 32 of these, third only to Clive Lloyd and Steve Waugh). He also played most Test innings (265) and scored most Test fifties (63). He is the only player to score 150-plus runs in both innings of a Test match, and before fellow Australians Mark Taylor and Mark Waugh overtook him he held the record for taking most catches (156). Also he had played the greatest number of Tests (156) before Steve Waugh eclipsed this record in the Caribbean in April 2003.

On a negative scale, Border is the only cricketer to make a duck in his first and 100th Tests. Like Lloyd, he was a prolific left-hand batsman, a superb fielder, an occasional bowler and a successful captain. However, that was where the similarity ended. Like Sunil Gavaskar before him and Steve Waugh after him, Border can best be measured on the weight of statistics. To all three, milestones were mountains which had to be scaled. Not that they were not attractive to watch in the middle. They had strokes for every occasion but seldom unleashed them. They knew their country depended on them. They dropped an anchor and let batsmen at the other end grab the limelight. They were there for durability and comfort, not for brilliance. They were the warm houses you wanted to come back to, not opulent seaside resorts with shimmering chandeliers and million-dollar views.

Mike Coward described Border in *Wisden 1995* as 'an unromantic, uncomplicated but uncompromising workman cricketer. He was an ordinary soul who accomplished extraordinary deeds.' John Woodcock echoed him in the London *Times*: 'Allan Border has not so much style as modus operandi. He is utterly practical.'

Born on 27 July 1955 in Cremorne, a waterside suburb in Sydney,

Allan Robert Border's family moved to adjoining Mosman where Allan played most of his cricket at junior, club and grade levels at the Mosman Oval, which was named after him in 1993. I first met Border when the Sydney branch of the Australian Cricket Society named him the NSW Young Cricketer of the Year in March 1977. The great Bill O'Reilly, then the Patron of the Society, told him, 'You have a special talent. You will be given much advice. My advice is not to follow any advice.' No wonder Border had that confused 'do I follow this advise or not?' look!

A self-effacing man of simple taste and joys, Border's Test debuts as a player and captain were traumatic. He came in the Australian team during the 'Packer era' when most of the stars had defected to World Series Cricket in the late 1970s. Bob Simpson, who had not played first-class cricket for a decade, had to be 'un-retired' to lead Australia successfully against India in 1977–78 and then tour the West Indies where they were thrashed. An inexperienced Graham Yallop took over as captain in 1978 and the rookie Aussies were trounced 1-5 by a full-strength Mike Brearley-led England. It was lambs to the slaughter.

The only consolation for Yallop's men was their victory in the third Test in Melbourne when Border made an inglorious debut; making 29 and 0 run-out. The home victory was thanks to a 10 wicket haul by paceman Rodney Hogg — playing in only his third Test and yet with 27 wickets in his bag after the match. In the following Test in Sydney which Australia lost, and with it the series, Border showed his steely temperament contributing an unbeaten 60 (only Rick Darling scored more) and a top score of 45 — unbeaten again — out of Australia's pathetic total of 111. It was a glimpse of the near future when Border became the Atlas of Australian cricket, a warhorse, the Rock of Gibraltar.

In the next Test in Adelaide, Australia was bundled out for 164 and 160, Border made 11 and 1 and was dropped for the final Test in Sydney. This was the only Test Border missed in his prolific international career spanning 17 years.

Border was forced to take up the Australian captaincy during an equally stressful period. After many summers of feuding, the Australian Cricket Board and World Series Cricket joined hands in 1981. Still the conflict as to who should lead Australia was not resolved. Should it be the experienced Greg Chappell, or the rookie Kim Hughes who had remained loyal to the ACB during their war with Kerry Packer. Besides, Chappell was choosy about countries he toured. Hughes was appointed captain against Clive Lloyd's all-

Border is out for a duck in his 100th Test. (*The Age*, Melbourne)

powerful West Indians in 1984–85. It was a mixed blessing, as Hughes was soon to realise. The Windies in the 1980s were arguably the strongest side to strut on a cricket field, staking comparison with Don Bradman's 1948 Invincibles. Against the lethal pace attack of Marshall, Garner and Holding, and an imposing batting line-up of Viv Richards, Lloyd, Greenidge, Haynes, Richardson and Gomes, Australia tasted humiliating defeats in Perth and Brisbane. It led to an emotion-choked Hughes tearfully resigning as captain and Border with a 'who, me?,' 'why me?' expression becoming a reluctant leader.

'On the one hand I was excited,' recalls AB in his autobiography, *Beyond Ten Thousand: My Life Story*, 'but on the other hand I was starting to think, "Oh, no!" Maybe this is not the time to cop this job, Allan … two down in the series, we've just lost the skipper and the media are using words like "Australian rabble!"' He had just watched Hughes' demise and thought: 'That's not for me. I'm really happy just playing. I don't need that sort of drama.'

Although gritty, he did not consider himself forceful enough as captain because he wanted to be one of the boys. Under the new skipper Australia lost in Adelaide and drew in Melbourne but won the Sydney Test. Two new faces, the New South Wales spin twins Bob 'Dutchy' Holland and Murray Bennett, took 15 wickets and the Australians surprised themselves by winning by an innings. A victory against a powerful team in only his third Test would have delighted any captain, but Border felt that in a way it was a hollow victory. The

Windies had already won the Frank Worrell Trophy 3-0 and did not appear hungry enough on a turning tract.

For the next two seasons it was a rough ride for AB. Australia kept losing, and after succumbing meekly to England in the Melbourne Test of December 1986 and surrendering the Ashes Bill O'Reilly wrote in the *Sydney Morning Herald*: 'As wooden spooners we are top-liners. Nobody threatens a position in the mullock heap at the bottom of the ladder. We flounder supreme.'

Border hit back by beating the Poms in the final Test of the series in Sydney, thanks to Dean Jones' magnificent century and the spin-duo of debutant Peter Taylor and Peter Sleep. Still the doubters remained unconvinced. Wrote Keith Miller: 'One of the first things I learnt was that if you can't be a good cricketer then try to look like one. Look at Border; sleeves rolled down, scruffy beard, hand on the chin. He looks more like an escapee from a Ned Kelly gang movie. He stands in the slips scratching his beard or his bottom and offers his players no encouragement.'

Strong words. Cruel words. If Border was hurt at such vitriolic comments he did not show it. Then a mini miracle. All the doom and gloom of Australian cricket disappeared in nine months. Gone was Border's beard and his bum-scratching. The little-fancied Australians won the 1987 World Cup in India and Border was proclaimed a hero and a saviour. Prior to this World Cup, he had lost weight by giving up fast food and reducing his beer intake. He smiled more, grunted less. A cartoonist called him a 'born again Border.' The best thing to happen to Australia during that tour to India was not so much to win the World Cup as to do well despite Border failing with the bat.

Before this it was heart-breaking for him to score consistently but before he could unstrap his pads, so to speak, the rest of Australian batting caved in. Too often, another batting triumph for AB coincided with another loss for Australia. He threatened to resign as captain on several occasions. However, in India in 1986 as also during the World Cup next season, David Boon and Geoff Marsh gave Australia steady starts and middle order batsmen Dean Jones, Steve Waugh and Mike Veletta thrashed the attack. This relaxed Border as he could think out strategies with a cool, helmet-less head. He contributed to Australia's seven-run victory against England in the World Cup final at Eden Gardens, Kolkata, by scoring 31 runs and taking 2 for 38. This included the prize scalp of rival captain Mike

Gatting, out attempting a reverse sweep when in fine touch at 41. To the delight of 85,000 Kolkata fans their adopted hero — Border — took a lap of honour along with his team-mates. This victory was one of the highlights of his distinguished career.

'The Reliance [World] Cup was one helluva tough trophy,' remembers Border in *Beyond Ten Thousand*. 'It survived a victory lap of Eden Gardens and the shenanigans of long, dressing room celebrations, although if you ever get the chance to look it over in the Cricket Board trophy cabinet you'll notice there are a couple of diamonds missing from the cricket ball-like spheres that top it.'

Other memorable moments in Allan 'Pugsley' Border's cricket career included receiving the Order of Australia and the next day being feted by tens of thousands of fellow Australians; the tied Test at Chennai, India, in 1986; the tickertape parade turned on by Sydneysiders in September 1989 after Australia's Ashes winning triumph in England; and passing Sunil Gavaskar's Test aggregate record of 10,122 runs in the Christchurch Test of February 1993 — the record he still holds and cherishes.

The highest aggregate man, Border, received a fine compliment from the highest average superstar, Sir Donald Bradman. 'I was pleased to learn that Allan Border has now become the highest scorer in Test cricket. Not only does this recognise his skill as a batsman, it is also a tribute to his physical fitness and tough character because it has taken many years of toil to reach such a milestone. Australians look upon Border as a typical Aussie battler who has served his country well.'

The four he hit off Dipak Patel to surpass Gavaskar gave AB an even bigger buzz than the sweep shot he put through a Mosman bathroom window at the age of 13. When he climbed through a broken window to retrieve the ball, he was confronted by the first nude woman he had seen in his life.

His 100th Test which was against the West Indies at the MCG, started on 24 December 1988. As Border was the first Australian to make 100 Test appearances, there was a fair deal of publicity in the media. Before play commenced on Christmas eve, he was presented with a Waterford crystal by the Australian Cricket Board. This complemented a small teddy bear he had received from his four-year-old son, Dene, as an early Christmas gift.

Border won the toss and sent the Windies in to bat. The pitch had a greenish tinge and as Australia had already lost the first two Tests,

Border had to do something different and adventurous. As the Australian bowlers captured eight of the best batsmen for 199, Border's gamble was justified. However, the tailenders Curtly Ambrose and Courtney Walsh, known more for their killer instinct as fast bowlers rather than match-saving batsmen, came to the visitors' rescue. At stumps on the opening day, the West Indies were 8 for 246 — neither side in a commanding position. Border's contribution was two catches, including his 110th in Test annals when he caught Viv Richards who was playing his 102nd Test. The ACB Chairman Malcolm Gray threw a party for the Australian team under a marquee on the extensive lawn of his elegant Melbourne home. The team celebrated Christmas with their loved ones.

The visitors were bowled out for 280 on Boxing Day after Ambrose (44) and Walsh (30 not out) had added a face-saving 57 runs for the ninth wicket. With Australia at 3 for 117, emerged Border at 5.24 p.m. to bat, the eighth cricketer and first Australian to play 100 Tests. He was given a standing ovation by over 26,000 MCG fans as he reached the batting crease. Unfortunately, he lasted only eight minutes and five balls. Ambrose, the Windies express and the nemesis of world-class batsmen, spoilt Border's celebrations with two unplayable yorkers in the space of six balls. He bowled Border for a duck and undermined the confidence of a struggling Dean Jones.

Border's dismissal for a nought in his historic Test kept sub-editors busy as the Australian captain reluctantly hogged the wrong sort of headlines: 'Border's Day is Curtly Curtailed' (*Sydney Morning Herald*), 'Fate Deals Border the Cruelest Blow' (*The Australian*), 'AB Duck is Bitter Pill to Swallow' (*Daily Telegraph*).

Rod Nicholson wrote in the next day's *Daily Telegraph*: 'Oh, Allan! What a celebratory catastrophe at the MCG yesterday! He didn't have tears in his eyes when he took block but if he didn't when he was bowled by Ambrose, certainly the Australian cricket public did.'

It was the 'Duck of the century,' according to a caption under a picture of Border with bails flying in the *Sydney Morning Herald*.

The clock unhappily turned back a full 100 Tests for Border who was out for a duck in his Test debut, also at the MCG, a decade previously. He has never forgotten that disastrous opening as he will not forget this 'duck of the century,' only his fifth nought in a career then spanning 174 Test innings. Since his last zero — c. Randall b. Willis 0 in Brisbane against England in November 1982, his 47th Test — Border had scored 4435 runs in 52 Tests and 89 innings. Only England's David

AB talking straight with a journalist, beer in hand. *(K.M.-H.)*

Gower, AB's close friend, had played more Test innings (99) without recording a duck. 'But no other batsman has scored so heavily between ducks,' wrote Mike Coward in the *Sydney Morning Herald*. 'And twice when he failed to score, he was run out.' He had made ducks in his first, 30th and 47th Tests (all against England) and against New Zealand in his 41st.

This was his first duck against the West Indies. Naturally, he was crestfallen when he cut his way through the silence to the pavilion. His first thoughts were more for Australia's predicament than his personal disappointment. Although averaging a healthy 52.75 in his Test career thus far, he had managed only 77 runs in the series at a sickly average of 15.40. 'Border's failure in his 100th Test will become part of the lore of the game,' wrote Mike Coward. 'For a Border duck is even rarer than a Bradman duck.'

Terry Brindle was more eloquent in *The Australian*: 'Fate and Curtly Ambrose smacked Allan Border in the teeth in cricket's modern equivalent of the square ring last night. The cavernous MCG greeted Border's entry as a batsman into his hundredth Test match with the rapture which fight fans reserve for champion pugilists; not least those whose durability earns them the nickname of "Pugsley" ... Border's dismissal had the trappings in human terms of Greek tragedy, a grand opera or a sharp instrument across the jugular.'

Eulogised Terry Smith in the *Daily Telegraph Mirror* in 1993: 'When Allan Border dies, the inscription on his gravestone should simply say, "He was at his best when the chips were down." With an icy look and stubble in his chin, AB has shored up the Australian innings so many times with a counter attack that it has become his trademark.'

Rating for 100th Test: 1/10.

9 Kapil Dev

Kapil Dev is unique. The only Indian fast bowler to dominate the international scene for over a decade, he is the only all-rounder to achieve the Test double of 5000 runs and 400 wickets, the youngest to do the 1000 runs and 100 wickets Test double, and the first all-rounder to play 100 Test matches. In July 2002 he was chosen by a panel of 32 international judges (cricketers, writers and broadcasters) as the *Wisden* Indian Cricketer of the Century ahead of legends Vinoo Mankad, Sunil Gavaskar and Sachin Tendulkar.

The 1980s have been recognised as a decade of all-rounders with New Zealander Richard Hadlee, Pakistan's Imran Khan, England's Ian Botham and Kapil vying for top honours. All four were outstanding cricketers, with Hadlee and Imran better bowlers and Kapil and Botham entertaining crowds with their lofty hitting.

Kapil held the record of being the most prolific wicket-taker (434 wickets in 131 Tests) till West Indian quickie Courtney Walsh (519 wickets) and Australian leg-spinner Shane Warne (491) overtook him with Sri Lankan spinner Muttiah Muralitharan hot on their heels. To be a fast bowler and an Indian sounds like an oxymoron but Kapil succeeded on lifeless Indian pitches with dedication and natural talent. Not as sizzling fast as Tyson, Hall, Marshall, Ambrose, Thomson, Shoaib or Lee, Kapil swung the ball like a boomerang and his snaky breakback that struck with the speed of a cobra.

Gavaskar remembers Kapil's debut in the Faisalabad Test in October 1978. Sadiq Mohammad was a seasoned opener for Pakistan and came out to bat in the national green cap. 'No need for helmets, we're playing India,' he said to himself. Wrong! 'He had a scare as a

Have bat, will win World Cup, says Kapil Dev.
(Courtesy G.E. Features)

Kapil bouncer whistled past his head with the kind of hiss only those who have faced deliveries of that speed can hear,' Gavaskar recalled. Sadiq asked for a helmet pronto! Just as well. In the next over another bouncer from Kapil hit Sadiq flush on his helmet and went for four byes. Imagination boggles, had Sadiq not worn the helmet. Kapil had arrived and he stayed on the Test scene for 16 years. India at long last had found a bowler who could deliver knockout punches. He also scored 59 as a night watchman in that match and a quality all-rounder had emerged.

Kapil Dev Nikhanj was born in Chandigarh, Hariyana, on 6 January 1959 (give or take a few years, as Kapil himself is not sure). Gavaskar was among the first to spot his talent. Kapil is a rare jewel. Like Keith Miller, Garry Sobers, Mankad and Botham, he can be included in a team as a bowler or as a batsman. As he was a world record-holder in taking most Test wickets till the last millennium, he is considered more of a bowler than a batsman. In future, however, he may be remembered equally for his carefree and exhilarating batting and his six appeal, for he was a mighty tonker of sixes. To him bowling was a serious job, he was often a one-man demolition squad whose job it was to dismiss batsmen — day in and day out — from 1978 to 1994. Batting, however, was a relaxation. He stood tall and hit tall; he loved his sixomania and shared his exuberance with spectators. 'Test cricket is for batsmen, not bowlers,' he once said. 'Bowlers are like slaves.' His bowling restricted and troubled batsmen but his batting enchanted and often won matches, especially the 1983 World Cup.

Oddly, his careless batting led to his being dropped in a Test after playing 66 Tests in a row from October 1978 to December 1984. Subsequently he played 65 consecutive Tests from January 1985 to March 1994. The Kolkata Test of December–January 1984–85 was the only gap in his 131 Test career. He was blamed for India's eight-wicket defeat by England in the previous Test in Delhi when he played a risky shot when prudence was the key word. Selectors, when will they learn? To expect Kapil to bat defensively is equivalent to asking a Formula One driver to keep to a speed limit of 60 kmh. The Indian selectors are known for their short memories. It was Kapil's daredevil hitting which led to his country's finest hour — India winning and lifting the World Cup at Lord's on 25 June 1983 under his captaincy.

Prior to 1982, he was a bowler who could bat. His Test batting average overseas was a pathetic 13. He announced himself as a batsman on the tour of England where he played sizzling innings of 41, 89, 66 and 97. Every time, he appeared likely to score the fastest century in Test history, then he got out. In the Lord's Test India was tottering at 5 for 45 when in walked Kapil with his characteristic swagger and made 41. India was forced to follow on and Kapil defended for a while with Dilip Vengsarkar. Soon Kapil broke loose and smashed 89 runs out of 117 added in a mere 15 overs. His 89 adventurous runs included three sixes and 13 fours. The quickest century was his for the taking when Botham had him caught at short mid-wicket. Kapil also bagged eight wickets (5 for 125 and 3 for 43), a marvellous all-round performance.

Not quite satisfied, he reached 50 in 33 minutes in the second Test at Manchester — overdrives predominating. In the third and final

All-round excellence. Kapil Dev with Garry Sobers. *(K.M.-H.)*

Test at The Oval, India faced the follow-on but Kapil did the rescue act — again — by savaging 97 runs off just 92 balls in 102 minutes, slashing two sixes and 14 fours. India had lost her 'dull dog' image thanks to Kapil Dev, 'the Hariyana Express.'

Between this Test series and the 1983 World Cup, Kapil played county cricket for Northamptonshire. His clear and tall hitting reminded the Northants spectators of Colin Milburn, a big hitter alas no longer with us. Kapil was named as one of the Five Cricketers of the Year in *Wisden* 1983, 'his all-round displays of rubbery exuberance' emphasised.

Kapil's best was to come a year later. Appointed as captain of India, he went on to win for India her only World Cup. No-one had given India a chance to make it to the semi-final but the match against lowly Zimbabwe lifted their spirit. 'Today Zimbabwe, tomorrow the world,' was how Kapil's men felt. India's World Cup record was woeful, having won only one match in 1975 and none in 1979. However, they started the 1983 campaign well by defeating the mighty West Indies in the opening round.

They had to beat the L-plated Zimbabweans to enter the semi-final. Batting first, India was 4 for 9, their acclaimed openers Gavaskar and Srikkanth out for ducks. Kapil entered, his usual toothy smile missing. India lost her fifth wicket for 17 in the 13th over. Put Kapil in a corner and he fights like a tiger. 'Leave it to me,' he told his batting partners as he added valuable runs with Roger Binny and Madan Lal and then an incredible 126 with Syed Kirmani (24) for the unbroken ninth wicket — a World Cup record. From a disastrous 5 for 17, India had recovered to a healthy 8 for 266, Kapil recording an unbeaten 175 with six sixes and 16 fours. It was then the highest score in a limited-overs international and still regarded as one of the most spectacular innings in any form of cricket. The Zimbabweans batted courageously but fell 31 runs short.

Inspired by this narrow win, India went on to beat Australia in a qualifier, England in the semi-final and met West Indies, the winners of the previous two World Cups, in the final. Sent in to bat, India was dismissed for 183. An easy win for the Windies was on the cards but Kapil Dev and his medium-pacers had different ideas. 'Master Blaster' Viv Richards and Desmond Haynes took the score to 1 for 50. Haynes was dismissed but Richards kept attacking. He lifted Madan Lal for what appeared to be a six but Kapil ran like an Olympian and caught it. This was the turning point, the crucial catch had tilted the game India's way. Incredibly, India won by 43 runs and nearly 10,000 Indian supporters gathered around Lord's pavilion to cheer their heroes. Back in India there were all-night celebrations and a holiday was declared the next day.

Kapil was the national hero, an international superstar. The following year, West Indies extracted revenge by routing India in one-dayers and the Test series and Kapil lost his captaincy. Fortunately Kapil, the rustic with a simple smile, had his feet on the ground in moments grand and ignoble and carried on playing with the same spontaneous verve.

In November 1989, against Pakistan at Karachi, Kapil became the first non-specialist batsman to play 100 Tests. R. Mohan wrote in *Sportstar* (India), 'There was an air of celebration to the Karachi Test besides the regular competitive spirit. Kapil Dev was being feted left and right for his hundredth Test appearance. There was a genuine feeling of warmth for a person accomplishing such a feat … The charming thing about his 100th appearance was that the Pakistani organizations connected with the cricket that came up with many commemorative plaques.' Pakistan International Airlines was the first to come up with a lovely silver salver for Kapil on the eve of the Test. The Board of Control for Cricket in Pakistan followed, and so did Habib Bank of Pakistan. The Indian Board also presented a silver plaque to Kapil at the team meeting before the Test.

Kris Srikkanth won the toss and sent Pakistan in to bat. Pakistan made 409, Imran hitting an unbeaten 109 and Javed Miandad, playing his 98th Test, scored 78. Kapil, despite being fortified by commemorative plaques, bowled with his customary fire on his special day to capture 4 for 69 in 24 overs while the medium-pacer Manoj

Prabhakar took 5 for 104. Both were helped by Mohammad Azharuddin, who accepted five brilliant catches.

India started badly and was in strife at 6 for 85 but was rescued by Kapil (55) and Ravi Shastri (45) who added 78 runs for the seventh wicket. Then the little wicket-keeper Kiran More scored an unbeaten 58 and India totalled 262, still 147 runs in arrears. Pakistan went for quick runs (Salim Malik 102 not out, Shoaib Mohmmad 95) but Kapil restricted their run-rate, his analysis being 36-15-82-3 as he swung the ball appreciably. Thus he took seven out of 15 wickets to fall, and he had dismissed quality batsmen Aamer Malik, Shoaib Mohammad and Javed Miandad twice each and Shahid Saeed once. When capturing his third wicket in the first innings, he became the fourth bowler to take 350 Test scalps. India was challenged to make 453 runs to win and was 3 for 303 at stumps. Kapil did not get a chance to bat in the second innings of the drawn Test. It was a Test to remember for him, 55 runs, seven wickets and four shining plaques.He went on to play 31 more Tests and set records, as mentioned earlier. A year after his 100th Test he played a cameo role in the Lord's Test against England. Now remembered as the Graham Gooch Test (he made 333 and 123), India needed 24 runs to avoid the follow-on with only tailender Hirwani at the other end. Kapil got those 24 runs in four balls, four successive sixes off Eddie Hemmings.

Kapil was an energiser; batting, bowling or fielding for 16 years. In 131 Tests he scored 5248 runs at 31.05, hitting eight centuries (163 being his highest) and 27 fifties. He also snared 434 wickets at 29.65 taking five wickets in an innings 23 times and 10 wickets in a Test twice, and held 64 catches. His best bowling was 9 for 83 against West Indies at Ahmedabad in 1983–84. Bowling was his wife, his life, his 10 to 6 job, his bread and butter. Batting was his mistress, his indulgence. He seldom strayed when bowling and hardly ever batted with a straight bat; his cross-bat flings giving spectators almost orgasmic delight.

Rating for 100th Test: 6/10.

10 Javed Miandad

Javed Miandad was a controversial cricketer, talented, prolific and mixed-up. He had the ego of Mohammad Ali, the belligerence of John McEnroe and the majestic stroke-play of Greg Chappell. He had that certain presence, almost an aura. He was a magnet which attracted and repulsed — depending on your polarity.

Among his contemporaries, only Viv Richards had his dazzling array of strokes, spirit of adventure and cocky arrogance. A man of many words, he did not exactly say 'I am the greatest,' but implied it. He annoyed team-mates (who once refused to play under him) and inspired them to supreme heights. He had a cheeky sense of humour. Bill Lawry recalls that during a Miandad innings in Australia, medium-pacer Merv Hughes — the one with walrus moustache — kept sledging him, saying that he was nothing but a 'Paki bus driver.' Ignoring Hughes, he scored an unbeaten century. As an exhausted Hughes was leaving the field after stumps were drawn, he felt a tap on his shoulder. Turning back he saw Miandad looking at him with his hand extended and saying, 'Ticket please.'

When Australians found it difficult to pronounce his name, he said 'Call me Me and Dad.' His on-field clash with Dennis Lillee in the 1981–82 Perth Test has become a part of cricket history. It kicked off a controversy that will be discussed for decades. Set a massive target of 543, Pakistan was 4 down for 100 when the ugly drama unfolded. Batting to Lillee, skipper Miandad turned the ball to the onside and was in the course of completing a single when he was obstructed by Lillee. The Aussie quickie kicked Miandad gently and the Pakistan captain responded by shaping to strike the kicker with the bat. They were separated by umpire Tony Crafter. Lillee was fined $200 and received a one-day international suspension. Miandad escaped scot-free. Although provoked, he was also responsible for this sordid saga.

Javed Miandad was born in Karachi on 12 June 1957, one of seven children. A batsman of rare, natural talent, he was commanding at the crease but often impetuous. He bowled quickish leg-spin and as a fielder he was a joy to watch. A prodigy, he made his first-class debut for Karachi as a 16-year-old in 1973–74. The following season he made 311 runs for Karachi Whites against National Bank in Karachi which remains his highest score in first-class cricket. Soon he made a memorable Test debut against New Zealand at Lahore in October 1976. At 19 years and 119 days, he became the youngest player to register a century on debut. Richard Hadlee bowled with hostility reducing Pakistan to 4 for 55 when the teenaged debutant was joined by the experienced Asif Iqbal. The youngster commanded authority and fluency from the very start of his magnificent innings. He reached his century in 170 minutes and had hit 21 fours in his 163 when he mistimed a pull through tiredness. He and Asif (166) had added 281 for the fifth wicket.

However, Miandad was not finished with the Kiwis yet. In the third Test in Karachi three weeks later he became the youngest to hit a Test double century. He was then 19 years and 141 days old and smacked 206 in 410 minutes which included two sixes and 29 fours. He scored 85 in the second innings, thus falling 15 runs short to join an elite group who scored a double century and a century in the same Test. The brash teenager had plundered 504 runs in the three-Test series to average 126 and was nicknamed 'Wonder Boy.' At 22 years and 260 days, he became the youngest Pakistani and the third youngest anywhere to lead his country. This was against Greg Chappell's Australians in Pakistan in 1979–80, the series Pakistan won 1-0.

On the same ground (Gadaffi Stadium, Lahore) where he had made his Test debut 13 years previously, Miandad became the first Pakistani to play 100 Tests. Always on the lookout for fresh challenges and dramatic effects, he was determined to shine— even if he had to sacrifice his aggressive stroke-play. He set his mind on emulating Colin Cowdrey, who was that far the only one to register a century in his 100th Test. He wanted to achieve what the likes of Boycott, Lloyd, Gavaskar, Gower, Richards, Vengsarkar, Border and Kapil had not.

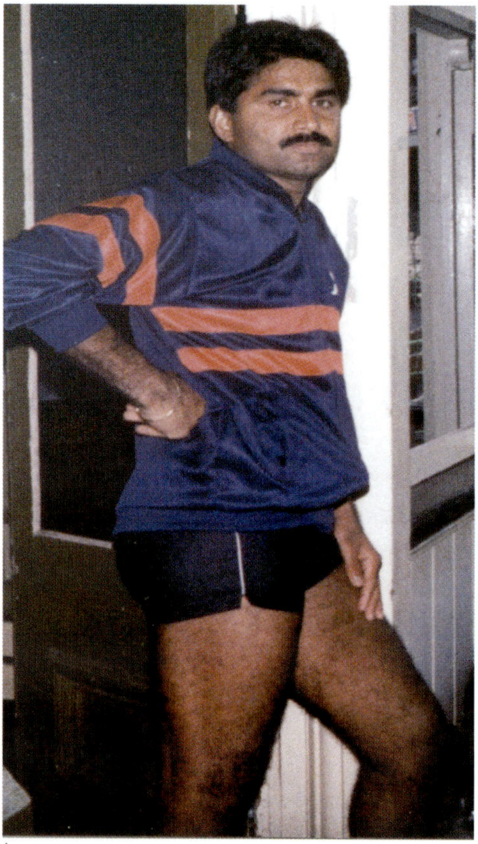

'Call me, Me and Dad,' says Javed Miandad. *(K.M.-H.)*

Miandad's 100th Test started on 1 December 1989 but he had to wait until the fourth day to go out to bat and the final day to realise his dream. On the morning of the opening day he was presented with a silver salver to commemorate the occasion. There was speculation in the press on his 'doing a Cowdrey' and he enjoyed the limelight. While others would find the pressure of expectations a burden, he lapped it up. As he waited and waited for his chance to bat, India piled on 509 runs, Sanjay Manjrekar striking 218 of the best. Pakistan's first target was to avoid the follow-on. Opening batsman Aamer Malik scored his second successive Test hundred. As Miandad went in to bat showing fierce determination, there was an unusual incident. English umpire John Holder suffered from a stomach upset and was replaced by Pakistani Khizar Hayat who stood at square-leg while John Hampshire umpired at both ends. Soon Shoaib Mohammad joined Miandad and attacked freely to outscore his batting partner. At stumps on day-4, Pakistan was 3 for 416, Miandad on 84, Shoaib 90. The normally aggressive Miandad had hit only three fours against younger Shoaib's 10 crispy fours.

Would Miandad add 16 runs to his score and join the great Cowdrey? He did, amid thunderous applause, taking in all 279 minutes. This was a dramatic moment for him and his country. It was his 22nd century, not his best but his sweetest. He soon hit out and was bowled by Ravi Shastri for 145, scored in 369 minutes off 291 balls and including 10 fours. During this historic innings, he passed Cowdrey's aggregate of 7629 runs (in 114 Tests) to become the sixth highest scorer in Test history. Also, he became the first player to

Miandad being presented with a silver salver on his 100th Test. (*Sportstar,* India)

record a century in his first and 100th Tests. The West Indies opening batsman Gordon Greenidge emulated this dual feat five months later. Shoaib went on to record a double century off the last ball of the match. But the hero was Miandad, the Wonder Boy who had turned into a maestro.

The heaviest scorer for Pakistan, Miandad went on to amass 8832 runs at 52.57 in 124 Tests, hitting 23 centuries, four of them double tons, with an unbeaten 280 (*v.* India at Hyderabad in 1982–83) as his highest. However, on 6 December 1989 he achieved cricket immortality. A man for all seasons, he held the record for scoring most runs in World Cup (1083 runs at 43.32 in 33 matches) until February 2003 when India's master bat Sachin Tendulkar went past him. Despite his successful debut and 100th Test, his 50-plus average in Tests (52.57) and first-class matches (53.44) and 40-plus average (41.70) in limited-overs internationals, he will be remembered for the conflicts and clashes, majestic stroke-play and supreme self-confidence.

Imran Khan, who captained Javed Miandad and also played under him, was apparently not his fan. Miandad's over-confidence often got up his nose. He wrote in *Imran: The Autobiography of Imran Khan* (1983): 'Javed does not take constructive criticism terribly well, he functions on instinct. It is so frustrating because he thrives on big match atmosphere yet is prone to impetuosity and attacks the bowlers too early … a real fighter, he has great guts yet loses concentration. He has tended to symbolise the strengths and defects of our batting in recent years [1980s], exotic stroke-play mixed up with suicidal tendencies.'

Rating for 100th Test: 7.5/10.

11 Gordon Greenidge

There are quite a few similarities between Gordon Greenidge and Javed Miandad. Both were innovative stroke-makers, adventurous and instinctive. Both are characters who entertained. Both shone out for their countries and for an English county (Greenidge for Hampshire, Miandad for Glamorgan). More pertinent to the book, they are the only cricketers to score centuries in their first and their 100th Tests.

Greenidge is considered one of the best opening batsmen of his time and certainly the most aggressive. Born in Barbados on 1 May 1951, Cuthbert Gordon Greenidge spent 14 years in his native Barbados before he migrated to Reading, England, in 1965 with his family. Soon he was in the school XI as a middle-order batsman, arousing interest with his powerful stroke-play. As a youngster he hated fielding but he trained hard including running on the streets at night (which on one occasion attracted police attention) and became an agile fielder. So alert, in 108 Tests he took 96 catches. A lazy lad, he worked hard for his success and during his first-class career spanning 23 summers from 1970 to 1992 he scored 37,354 runs at 45.88, hitting 92 centuries, his highest being 273 not out for D.H. Robins' XI *v.* Pakistanis at Eastbourne in 1974.

Greenidge was lucky to have three outstanding batsmen as his opening partners: Roy Fredericks and Desmond Haynes for the West Indies, and South African Barry Richards for Hampshire. Greenidge remembers his first pairing with Barry Richards. Against Warwickshire at Edgbaston, Birmingham, in August 1970 they put on 88 runs in the second innings, the 19-year-old Greenidge making an unbeaten 62 against quality bowlers David Brown and Lance Gibbs.

They won by nine wickets. In the next match, against Leicestershire at Southampton, Greenidge and Richards added 201.

'My philosophy [in batting] has always been to try and bury the ball into the wall of some distant building and the only way to do that is to hit it as hard as possible,' he wrote in *Gordon Greenidge: The Man in the Middle*. To him every ball bowled — even a good length delivery — was a bad ball. In 1972, he returned to Barbados to see what cricket, and life, had to offer and to try his luck. He was qualified to play for England and was good enough for Test selection but he opted to represent the West Indies. This despite the fact that in his early days he never felt at home in Barbados. Nor did his people think of him as one of them.

Selected to tour India, Sri Lanka and Pakistan in 1974–75, Greenidge made a stunning Test debut. It was also the first Test staged in Bangalore, the garden city. Greenidge won the Indians over by making 93 and 107. On a wet pitch carelessly left uncovered, the conditions were stacked against the visitors when they were sent in to bat by India's captain Mansur Ali Pataudi. Greenidge enjoyed beginner's luck, being twice let off before he had made 15. His opening partner, Fredericks, retired after spraining his ankle and Alvin Kallicharran joined Greenidge with the score on 38. They added 139 runs in even time. Greenidge was run out at 93 just before stumps on the first day. Despite a century by Kallicharran, the West Indies could total only 289. They managed a 29 run lead but started the second innings shakily. They were 3 for 75 and were rescued by Greenidge, who played a splendid knock of 107. With skipper Clive Lloyd blasting a spectacular 163, the awesome twosome added 207 runs and eventually won the match by 267 runs. Greenidge became the first West Indian to score a century on his Test debut overseas.

Subsequent to this marvellous start, Greenidge did little of note in the Indian subcontinent and much worse on the tour to Australia in 1975–76. He failed against the extra bounce and zip of Australian pitches which was exploited by Dennis Lillee and Jeff Thomson. He made a pair in the first Test in Brisbane, low scores of 3 and 8 in the Melbourne Test and was dropped from subsequent Tests. It taught him a lesson. 'It was the first time I had failed so miserably and it made me realise that batting in Test cricket was more than just crashing the ball about,' he recalls in his autobiography. 'I knew from that point that I had to tighten my game.'

They called Gordon Greenidge an axeman. 'In full flight he was a glorious sight, impossible to contain,' observed Peter Roebuck. *(Getty Images)*

He still hit bad balls furiously but his shot selection improved. One of his best series was against England in 1976. His 134 out of West Indies total of 211 in the Manchester Test on a pitch of uneven bounce was a lesson in dedication and good technique. It was crisis time as the Windies were 4 for 26 and Greenidge came to their rescue by scoring 63.51% of the total, second only to Charles Bannerman's record of scoring 67.35% of Australia's total in the inaugural Test in Melbourne way back in 1877. Then Michael Holding lived up to his nickname of 'The Whispering Death' by taking 5 for 17 in 14.5 deadly overs and England was rolled out for 71.

Greenidge continued from where he had left off in the first innings by hitting 101 in the second. He had valuable partnerships: 116 runs for the opening wicket with Fredericks and 108 for the second wicket with Viv Richards. The Windies declared at 5 for 411 and won by 425 runs — their biggest victory over England. In this Test, Greenidge became the second West Indian after the legendary George Headley to register two centuries in a Test against England. Incidentally, Headley achieved this twice against England, in 1929–30 and in 1939. Greenidge's dual tons were preceded by an invaluable 84 out of 182 in the previous Test at Lord's and followed by another century, 115, at Leeds; his third consecutive Test hundred. In five Tests, he amassed 592 runs at 65.77 and ended the tour by belting the fastest century of the season. Against Nottinghamshire at Trent Bridge he reached his ton in 69 sparkling minutes.

Despite his successes, Gordon Greenidge's dismal record in Australia in 1975–76 rankled. He took his revenge against his tormentors by recording his highest score in the Bridgetown Test of April 1991. In the previous three Tests in the series, he had scored measly 69 runs at 23.00. As he made 10 in the first innings in Bridgetown, he had managed 79 runs at 19.75. Australia replied weakly to the home team's 149 and trailed by 15 runs. Then it was Greenidge at his belligerent best. Eleven days short of his 40th birthday, and his place in doubt, he played a grand, chanceless inning of 226. It came off 478 deliveries in 686 minutes and he hit 31 fours. He shared partnerships of 129 with Haynes (49) for the opening wicket — their 16th century stand, 199 with Richie Richardson (99) and 102 with Carl Hooper (57). Greenidge was fourth out at 454 and eventually West Indies won by 343 runs. It was perhaps Greenidge's happiest Test in a career of many ups and a few downs. In 108 Tests, he scored 7558 runs at 44.72 with 19 centuries (four of them double hundreds) and took 96 catches. Technically a master against spin and pace, he attacked bowling with the crushing brutality of a tank.

Greenidge became the third West Indian to play 100 Tests. It was in the fifth and final Test against England at St John's, Antigua, in April 1990. After an engrossing series locked at 1-all, it was very one-sided. In the absence of an injured Graham Gooch, Allan Lamb captained England. Surprisingly, he opted to bat on the fastest and bounciest pitch of the series. With Ian Bishop (5 for 84), Curtly Ambrose (2 for 79) and Courtney Walsh (3 for 51) bowling bouncers galore, England was skittled out for 260.

Greenidge, who was presented with a silver salver to mark his 100th Test appearance by the West Indies Board President Clyde Walcott before the match started, batted gloriously the next day. The magnificent Caribbean openers, Greenidge (149) and Man of the Match Haynes (167) overtook England's total by putting on 298 runs. It was the 14th century (and fourth double century) partnership for them in their 134th innings together. Their 298 run first wicket stand was a new West Indian record, their previous best against England was 206 by Fredericks and Lawrence Rowe at Kingston, Jamaica, in 1973–74. Greenidge shared his country's best opening stands against all the opponents: 296 (the previous overall record) with Haynes against

India at St John's in 1982–83, 250 (unbroken) also with Haynes against Australia at Georgetown in 1983–84, 225 again with Haynes against New Zealand at Christchurch in 1979–80 and 182 with Fredericks against Pakistan at Kingston, 1976–77.

Like Colin Cowdrey and David Gower before him, Greenidge also reached 7000 Test runs during his 100th Test. He passed Greg Chappell's 7110 to move into 11th place on the all-time list with 7134 runs. It was his 18th Test hundred and seventh against England. When it appeared that nothing could part the prolific partnership of Greenidge and Haynes, Gladstone Small's bullseye throw from 70 metres ran out a disbelieving Greenidge. It was a marvellous innings which included three sixes and 18 fours from 207 balls in a stay of 380 minutes. His 149 runs remains the highest score by a cricketer playing his 100th Test.

The Windies took a 186 run lead and bounced out England for 154 to win the Test by an innings and the series 2-1. In the second knock, England had totalled only five more runs than Greenidge's individual innings and 13 fewer than Haynes! Greenidge appropriately ended the Test by catching Philip DeFreitas off Ambrose for nought. The Antiguan crowd, always among the world's noisiest, celebrated Greenidge's 100th Test in animated style.

According to Peter Roebuck in *Wisden 1992*, 'Born in the West Indies and raised in England, Greenidge had a foot in both camps and a tent in neither … In full flight, Greenidge was a glorious sight, and impossible to contain. So awesome was his power, so complete his authority, that once a bombardment was under way not a ball could be bowled to him … At his best, unleashed, he was intimidating.'

Rating for 100th Test: 7.5/10.

12 Desmond Haynes

Some names are integrally linked, viz. Romulus and Remus, Samson and Delilah, Simon and Garfunkel, Laurel and Hardy, Tom and Jerry …In cricket it is Hobbs and Sutcliffe, Worrell, Weekes and Walcott, Lawry and Simpson, Lillee and Thomson, Greenidge and Haynes.

Gordon Greenidge and Desmond Haynes opened the West Indies innings in a record 89 Tests. In 148 Test innings together, they accumulated 6483 runs at 47.32, having century partnerships a record 16 times and fifty-run stands on 26 occasions. Next best in number of Tests together are India's opening batsmen Sunil Gavaskar and Chetan Chauhan, 36 Tests, 59 innings, adding 3010 runs at 53.75 with 10 century and 10 fifty-run partnerships. Going by Robert Brooke's statistics from *Wisden 1992*, England's Jack Hobbs and Herbert Sutcliffe were the champion openers, adding 3249 runs at 87.81 in 25 Tests (38 innings) together and associated in 15 century and 10 fifty-run stands. Current Australian opening pair of Matthew Hayden and Justin Langer are fast catching up. As at 15 May 2003, they have played together in 24 Tests (40 innings together) adding 2669 runs at 68.44 and have been associated in nine century and eight fifty-run partnerships.

It was quite appropriate that Haynes scored a century in Greenidge's 100th Test, described in the previous chapter; Haynes (167) adding 298 runs with Greenidge (149) for the first wicket in the Antigua Test of April 1990. Unfortunately, Greenidge was not in the team for Haynes' 100th Test as he underwent an intricate knee surgery and retired shortly afterwards. Both were attractive stroke-players and superb technicians, although Haynes could drop anchor and play a defensive game. Haynes had a more extrovert personality than

Known as the 'silky assassin,' cricket was fun to Desmond Haynes. *(Getty Images)*

Greenidge. As Peter Roebuck wrote in *Wisden 1992*, 'To him [Haynes] cricket was a simple and spontaneous game, full of life and love and laughter. He could strike balls over cover, could run like a hare and hook with a sudden, quick, wristy movement. On his feet he was light, and as he collected his runs he was smiling, charming, crisp and flamboyant.' Frank Keating described Greenidge as the Cruel Axeman and Haynes as the Silky Assassin.

Desmond Leo Haynes was born in the Holders Hill district of Barbados on 15 February 1956, the eldest of three brothers. There was no cricket in the family but everyone in the area played this game. He made his first-class debut for Barbados in January 1977 and his first Test was against Australia the following season. In the Port-of-Spain Test on 3rd March 1978, Australia (weakened by their best players lost to World Series cricket) was shot out for 90 by the pace battery of Andy Roberts, Colin Croft and Joel Garner. The West Indies were left slightly more than an hour's batting before stumps on the opening day. In that time, openers Greenidge and Haynes unleashed such a flurry of shots that they smashed 79 runs off only 14 overs. On his Test debut, Haynes entertained a crowd of about 25,000 by hitting 20 runs off an over from speedster Jeff Thomson, including a hook for six, and by pulling spinner Jimmy Higgs for another six in the last over of the day. In that period, he also hit six fours. Thus he had scored 36 runs out of his unbeaten 53 in boundary hits. The pace was less hectic the following morning as the Australians bowled tight, Haynes adding only eight runs to score 61 of the 87 runs added for the first of their 148 Test innings in tandem.

It was a promising start to a prolific Test career. In 116 Tests, he amassed 7487 runs at 42.30 which included 18 centuries, with 184 runs against England at Lord's in 1980 as his highest. This was then the highest score by a West Indian at Lord's, breaking tour manager Clyde Walcott's record of 168 not out in 1950. (Haynes' record was broken by his partner Greenidge who made an unbeaten 214 in the 1984 Lord's Test.) In his innings of 184 in the rain-affected Lord's Test of 1980, Haynes showed phlegmatic temperament and superb range of strokes. He batted for almost eight hours and hit 27 fours and a six. After adding 223 runs for the second wicket with Viv Richards (145), Haynes added 51 with Alvin Kallicharran and 107 in 88 dazzling minutes with skipper Clive Lloyd (56). In reply to West Indies' imposing total of 518, England made 269 and 2 for 133.

One of his best innings was his 125 in the fifth and final Test against England at The Oval in 1984. It was a fluctuating match which the Windies won by 172 runs, securing the series 5-0. With Ian Botham taking 5 for 72, the visitors were dismissed for 190. But they hit back, bowling out England for 162, Malcolm Marshall finishing with 5 for 35. The Test took another twist as Greenidge, Larry Gomes and Richards were back in the pavilion and the score was 3 for 69. Haynes was passing through a bad patch, having scored only 100 runs at 16.67 in the previous four Tests. As he made only 10 in the first innings, his confidence must have been at an all time low. He had reserved his best, however, for when his country needed him. He batted for over seven hours to score a gritty 125 out of the team total of 346 and was adjudged Man of the Match. Set 375 to win, England could muster only 202.

My favourite Haynes innings was in the Sydney Test of January 1989. The West Indies had already won the series 3-0 and tended to play recklessly on a spinning track. The exception was Haynes, who gave his all, using his feet like a ballet dancer and top-scored in both innings. With trusted partner Greenidge (56), Haynes (75) gave the Windies a solid start of 90. The total was 1 for 144 and the Windies seemed on the way to a 'blackwash' when skipper Allan Border surprised everyone — including himself — by taking 7 for 46 with his left-arm spin. The Calypsos collapsed for 224 at stumps, losing their last nine wickets for only 80.

David Boon scored 149 out of Australia's 401 to take a 177-run lead. The Windies were in all sorts of trouble and were dismissed for 256. Haynes played a gallant and lone hand of 143 (55.86% of the total) as some of his partners unsuccessfully tried to smash Border and fellow-spinner Trevor Hohns for sixes. Haynes' 143 was considered by both captains — Richards and Border — as among the finest they had witnessed. He batted almost faultlessly for 315 minutes, assiduously smothering the spin and hitting only the loose deliveries. Australia won the Test by seven wickets, Man of the Match, Border, fittingly hit the winning run. He had scored 91 runs in the match (75 and 16 not out) and taken 11 wickets (7 for 46 and 4 for 50). But Haynes had contributed valiantly, top-scoring in both innings with 75 and 143. He was the man who stood on the spinning deck, whence all but he had fled.

Haynes' first double century in first-class matches came a few months later when representing Middlesex in county cricket. He scored an unbeaten 206 at Ukridge. The year 1990 was memorable for him. He scored over 2000 runs (2036 at 63.62) for Middlesex who won the County Championship and he was named both the Britannic Assurance and Nixdorf Middlesex Player of the year.

His 100th Test was played in July 1991, against England at Trent Bridge in Nottinghamshire. England made 300 and West Indies took a 97 run lead, Richards stroking 80, Gus Logie 78 and Marshall 67. Haynes started well, smacking three fours but was caught by Robin Smith off David Lawrence for 18 made off 26 balls in 38 minutes. England totalled 211, the highlight of the fourth day was provided not by the players but by a male streaker, dressed only in heavy black boots and a garbage bin over his head.

Not distracted, the Windies won the Test by nine wickets, thanks to an unbroken 114 run stand for the second wicket by Haynes and Richie Richardson. The final day was blustery but dry and Haynes and Richardson took the side to victory at the stroke of lunch at 1 p.m. Haynes' unbeaten 57 had come off 97 deliveries in 149 minutes and he had spanked six fours. In this, his 100th Test appearance, he passed 2000 runs against England during the second innings to become the sixth West Indian to do so after Garry Sobers, Richards, Greenidge, Rohan Kanhai and Lloyd. Being a team man, Haynes had the deep satisfaction of playing an important role in his country's overdue victory in his landmark Test.

The mighty West Indies openers had contrasting personalities. Greenidge was neat and tidy, Haynes blissfully disorganized. Haynes told Keating after his 100th Test, fingering the pendant at the neck inscribed 'LIVE, LOVE, LAUGH,' 'I only had to look across at Gordon's neat and organized corner and say to myself, "Man there's the true pro to aspire to." It was an honour to be second fiddle to him all those years.'

Rating for 100th Test: 4/10.

13 Ian Botham

Cricket has produced characters; W.G. Grace, Merv Hughes, Derek Randall, Javed Miandad, Greg Matthews and Shane Warne. And then there was Ian Botham, who, according to Sunil Gavaskar, was 'the craziest cricketer I have known.' Gavaskar should know. Not only were they worthy opponents (among the best opening batsmen of all time against probably the best all-rounder of his time) but they also played together for Somerset.

A character, yes, but crazy? Gavaskar, who idolised Botham, explains in his book *Idols*: 'In the [Somerset] dressing room, he [Botham] was an absolute terror because he could never sit still ... If he did not find anything to do, he would punch you on the arms, dip his teaspoon in a pot of hot, boiling water and while you were sitting unawares, he would try to cause burns on your hands with the spoon or just a lighted match stick.' Dressing room or dungeon?

Botham may have been a prankster off the field but he was a mighty warrior on it, irrepressible and cheerfully insubordinate. With another Test immortal Vivian Richards, he formed a flamboyant and in later stages an ungovernable partnership for Somerset. Richards had traces of arrogance and ego, Botham had no artifice. With Botham you got what you saw, a man without malice. Naughty but nice, about sums him up. Underneath the tough exterior, he cared for humanity. His marathon walks to raise funds for leukaemia sufferers have been exemplary. He was a great all-rounder and remains a good humanitarian.

He did not care about statistics but they have been breathtaking. In 102 Tests he scored 5200 runs at 33.55 with 14 centuries (highest 208) and took 383 wickets at 28.40 (capturing five wickets in an innings 27 times, 10 wickets in a Test four times, his best bowling

Ian Botham, a slam-bang, no-nonsense cricketer. *(Stamp Publicity)*

spell being 8 for 34) and took 120 catches. Thus he is the only cricketer to do the triple of 5000 runs, 300 wickets and 100 catches. But there is more! He was the quickest to accomplish the Test double of 1000 runs and 100 wickets (in only 21 Tests and within 25 months). He did the double of a century and five wickets in a Test innings an incredible five times. Garry Sobers and Mushtaq Mohammad are the next best with twice each. Once Botham scored a century and took 13 wickets in the same Test, which is unique. More important, he converted apparently lost Test matches into glorious victories.

Ian Terrence Botham was born in Heswall in Cheshire on 24 November 1955. He made an instant impact, his debuts in both one-day cricket and in the Test arena were impressive. At 18, he played his first important match for Somerset against Hampshire in a one-dayer in 1974. Shortly after arriving at the crease, when Somerset was 8 for 113, needing 183 to win, he was hit full in the mouth by a bouncer from West Indies fast bowler Andy Roberts. Botham bled profusely, eventually lost four teeth, but declined to leave the field. He hit two soaring sixes while making an unbeaten 45, guiding Somerset to a victory.

He took 5 for 74 on the first day of his Test debut against Australia at Nottinghamshire in July 1977. In his second Test at Leeds, he again shone, capturing 5 for 21 off 11 economical overs in the first innings as England won to lead the series 3-0. Cricketers reach truly great status when a match is named after them. At least two Tests are called 'Botham's Test.' One was against India in Mumbai in 1980, while the drama-packed topsy-turvy 1981 Leeds Test against Australia the following year was the second.

Botham ('Both' to his friends and fans and 'Gorilla' to his victims) played perhaps his finest Test match in the Golden Jubilee Test in Mumbai in February 1980. His feat of scoring a century and taking 13 wickets has remained unparalleled in the 127-year history of Test cricket. On the opening day, he captured 6 for 58 to dismiss India for 242 (helped by wicket-keeper Bob Taylor who in all gloved seven catches). Botham came in to bat with England in trouble, 5 down for 58. Unconcerned, he added 171 runs with Taylor (43), scoring 114 runs in 206 resolute minutes which included 17 fours. He got better each day as he captured 7 for 48 (for amazing match figures of 13 for 106) to rout India for 149 and England won by 10 wickets with a day to spare. His versatility was in full bloom. He touched rock bottom next season, only to rise to everlasting fame. Despite his all-round excellence, his captaincy record was poor. He was too much of an individual to lead a team, too undisciplined to impose authority. It was darkest before the dawn for the beleaguered captain 'Both' in the Ashes series against Australia in 1981. Under him, Australia lost the first Test, he made a pair in the second Test and lost captaincy to Mike Brearley. This was, to use a cliché, a blessing in disguise for Botham. It was as if iron chains had been removed from his body and the Gorilla was his old exuberant self.

The third Test at Headingley, Leeds, was the stuff miracles are made of. It was one of the most fascinating and bewilderingly fluctuating Tests. One up in the series, Australia declared at 9 for 401, John Dyson scored 102, skipper Kim Hughes 89 and Botham took 6 for 95, indicating his return to form as a bowler. Despite his 50, England was dismissed for 174 and forced to follow-on. They appeared sunk at 7 for 135, still 92 runs behind when Graham Dilley joined Botham. Amid rising tension, the two fast bowlers started the rescue act, adding 117 runs in 80 minutes, Dilley contributing 56 precious runs. Botham refused to budge as he added 67 more runs with tailender Chris Old and remained unbeaten with 149 out of England's respectable total of 356. Still the win target for Australia was only 130 runs. It appeared easily achievable when the visitors reached 1 for 56. Just then tall Bob Willis, inspired by Botham's heroic deeds, struck crippling blows by grabbing 8 for 43 and England incredibly won by 18 runs. Botham had made it all happen scoring 199 runs and capturing seven scalps in this epic thriller.

Still not satisfied, Botham took 5 for 11 off 14 overs (9 maidens) in the second innings of the next Test in Birmingham which England won to lead 2-1 in the series. Botham was adjudged Man of the Match for the second Test in a row. He wasn't quite finished with the Aussies yet though. In the following Test in Manchester, England was tottering at 5 for 104 but then came Botham with his pocket full of miracles. He smashed 118 in 123 minutes off 102 balls, with six sixes (three off Dennis Lillee) and 13 fours. He completed his century with a six as England totalled 404 and won her third Test in succession to retain the Ashes. In the final Test at The Oval, a draw, he took 6 for 125 and 4 for 128. What a series for him — especially the last four Tests when he amassed 365 runs at 52.14 (with two tons) and took 28 wickets at 19.68 (with three five wickets per innings hauls and 10 for 253 in the final Test).

After this superhuman effort, everything Ian Botham did appeared as an anti-climax. His love for fast food made him put on pounds and his hunger for runs and wickets diminished somewhat as he approached his 100th Test. This was against New Zealand in the third and final Test in Wellington in February 1992. He was not included in the original XII, but was brought back in the side due to injuries to opening bowlers Derek Pringle and Chris Lewis. England batted first and scored 305 mainly through Alec Stewart's 107. Botham, appearing rusty, was caught by Chris Cairns off Murphy Su'a for 15. With centuries from John Wright and Andrew Jones, New Zealand declared at 9 for 432; Botham's figures being 14-4-53-1, dismissing the dangerous Cairns who was caught behind by Robert Russell. Going for a 3-0 whitewash England declared at 7 for 359, Allan Lamb striking 142 and Botham succumbing to the off-spin of Dipak Patel for a single. Botham shared the new ball with the unfortunate David 'Syd' Lawrence (whose injury in this Test ended his Test career) and took two of the three Kiwi wickets to fall for 53. 'Both' had dismissed both the openers, Blair Hartland (lbw for 19) and Wright (caught by Russell for 0) to have figures of 2 for 23.

Botham was now approaching 37 and was no more the charging rhino he was in his heyday. As a colt he was aggressive and brash — steaming in and blasting out batsmen with a splendid out-swinger. At his peak he was a hell-raiser in the middle and in the dressing room with his 'weapons of mass destruction,' bouncers, sixes, superheated spoons and lighted matches! However, wear and tear took their toll and the old devil lost his horns. Describing his last seasons, John Woodcock wrote in *Wisden 1994*: 'But his batteries were pretty nearly run down by then [1993], and once the England selectors were not interested in him they went flat ... His final days [in cricket] were more melancholy than misty-eyed.'

Rating for 100th Test: 2/10.

14 Graham Gooch

Stoic, unflappable, moustached and prolific. This is how spectators saw Graham Gooch from a distance. After chatting with him in the SCG press box during the January 2003 Ashes Test, I have to add one more adjective: friendly. Almost effusive with old friends. There was so much noise and laughter when Mike Gatting and David Lloyd greeted him that Australia's media manager Brian Murgatroyd had to appeal for peace and quiet: 'This is a working area for journalists, please keep noise to the minimum.' Gooch also appears smaller now. Perhaps distance had lent weight. Or had he lost ounces as he busily promoted his anti-baldness treatment around Australia?

Mention the name Gooch to a cricket-lover and he will remember his two doubles: a pair in his Test debut (against Australia at Birmingham in 1975) and his triple century and century in the same Test (*v.* India at Lord's in 1990). However, Gooch is more than a double or nothing person. His record at all levels is staggering. He remains the most prolific Englishman at Test level, having scored 8900 runs at 42.58 in 118 Tests, and at one stage he was the third highest scorer in Tests after Allan Border and Sunil Gavaskar.

According to English statistician, Robert Brooke, Gooch is the most prolific run-getter at first-class and international limited-overs levels. At the time of his retirement on 23 July 1997 (on his 44th birthday), Gooch had scored 65,933 runs at 45.81 if one added his 21,087 runs in top-level limited-overs matches to his first-class aggregate of 44,846 runs at 49.01. (Sir Jack Hobbs comes next with 61,237 runs at 50.65). Also Gooch remains the only one to record 2000 or more runs in a season five times since 1969 (in 1984, 1985, 1988, 1990 and 1993).

Apart from being a run-machine, Gooch was also an entertainer. As Christopher Martin-Jenkins summed up in *Wisden 1998*, he was 'a bold and imposing player, a mighty driver and fierce square-cutter, who looked at the crease to be taller and bulkier than he actually was, with a bat apparently broader than the law permits.' Until 1974, Gooch was without moustache, his trademark in later years, and very quiet. So quiet that his Essex captain Keith Fletcher wondered: 'Does *it* speak?' Mostly, he let his bat do the talking. Former England captain Ray Illingworth once remarked, 'The boy [Gooch] has the ability to go all the way. He is a big lad, hits the ball hard and crucially has time to play.' James Lawton of the *Daily Express* was so impressed with Gooch's 82 in 82 minutes against Cambridge University that he wrote: 'The boy with the build of a blacksmith has the classic fresh complexion and the image of a youthful contemporary of W.G. Grace.'

Born on 23 July 1953, Graham Alan Gooch was selected for MCC against the 1975 Australians under Ian Chappell. He made a lasting impression against the near lethal combination of Dennis Lillee and Jeff Thomson. MCC was on its knees at 3 for 11 when 21-year-old Graham hit a spirited 75 and added 109 runs with David Lloyd. Unfazed, the youngster hit Lillee through the covers with power and lifted Thomson and Gary Gilmour for sixes. This proved to be his passport to Test selection, which was against Australia in Birmingham. His debut was quite disastrous as he batted twice without getting a run: c. Rod Marsh b. Max Walker 0; c. Marsh b. Thomson 0. Also, none of the established players took the newcomer under his wing and he felt like a frightened kid on his first day at school. He was given one more chance but after failing again in the next Test at Lord's he was excluded from the other Tests in the series.

'My worst fears were confirmed,' he wrote in *'Gooch: My Autobiography'* (1995). 'Although I was very disappointed on learning that I had been dropped, I was not suicidal. I was picked to score some runs and I had not come up with any; end of the story.' Not quite. It was just a wobbly beginning. After the selectors forgot him for three years, he returned to Test cricket as an opening batsman against Pakistan. He hit a polished 54 at Lord's in 1978 and did not look back. It was one triumph after another for the likable 'Goochie.' He hit 20 Test centuries, only Colin Cowdrey (22) and Geoff Boycott (22) had hit more Test tons among Englishmen.

Guffaws galore! 'Goochie' with fellow buccaneer Mike Gatting in the SCG press box, January 2003. Who says Gooch does not show emotions? *(K.M.-H.)*

The year 1990 was a special one for captain Gooch when he set two records which still stand. In the Lord's Test, India presented England with a glorious opportunity to amass a huge score. On a good pitch, Indian captain Mohammad Azharuddin won the toss and sent England in to bat. England must have said 'Thank you' and had scored 2 for 359 at stumps on the opening day. Skipper Gooch and Allan Lamb were unbeaten with 194 and 104, although Gooch was lucky to be dropped by wicket-keeper Kiran More when 36. Gooch carried on gloriously the following day, amassing 333 in 627 minutes off 485 balls, smashing three sixes and 43 fours. (By a coincidence this innings is detailed on page 333 of *Wisden 1991*.) It was the highest score at Lord's, the third highest by an Englishman in Tests and the sixth highest overall in Test cricket (now ninth highest). He had added 308 runs for the third wicket with Lamb and 192 for the fourth wicket with Robin Smith (100 not out) and declared at 4 for 653.

India did not buckle in under this onslaught and started confidently. Ravi Shastri scored a round 100 and Azharuddin chipped in with 121 but it was left to Kapil Dev to save a follow-on. India needed 24 runs to make England bat again with only no. 11 batsman Narendra Hirwani in. Kapil said, 'Leave it to me' and hit four sixes in four balls — a Test record — and the follow-on was averted. Not quite satisfied with his first innings triple ton, Gooch hit another century in the second innings, his 123 came off 148 minutes and 113 balls and included four sixes and 13 fours. In this Test he had batted for 775 minutes, faced 598 deliveries and belted seven sixes and 56 fours to total 456 runs; a record still unmatched. (Australia's captain Mark Taylor came close in the Peshawar Test against Pakistan in

1998–99, scoring 334 not out and 92; a total of 426.)

On his triple century, Gooch appeared stoical as ever, 'no tap-dancing on the table,' he recalled. 'I wasn't going to destroy my reputation among the media people for being a dour old misery-guts.' When asked at the press conference how he felt, he predictably muttered, 'Okay, I suppose.' In his autobiography, he considered his 333 as among the best innings he had played.

His father, Alf, appeared as low key and blasé about his son's 456 runs in the Lord's Test — a family trait. But mum, Rose, was ecstatic. 'Oh, I think this is the best day of all. I mean 300, it's so special isn't it? I won't forget this day ever.'

With another century (116) in the next Test at Manchester and 85 and 88 in the third Test at The Oval, Gooch the run-glutton had amassed 752 runs at 125.33 in three Tests. As he had scored 306 runs in three Tests against New Zealand in the twin series, he had totalled 1058 runs at 96.18 in six Tests. He remains the only player to record more than 1000 Test runs during an English season. The paradox of the season was that in the first Test of the dual series at Nottingham, he was out for a golden duck — his first — lbw to Richard Hadlee. More than the runs accumulated, what pleased Gooch was that, under, him England won both the series.

Experts rank his unbeaten 154 in the second innings of the 1991 Leeds Test against the West Indies as his finest knock. England had managed a narrow 25 run lead when skipper Gooch opened England's second innings. With Curtly Ambrose bowling with fire, England lost wickets regularly. Twice Ambrose was on a hat-trick as wickets tumbled regularly. Gooch, however, remained unbeaten and untroubled as he carried his bat and scored 61% of runs. England won the Test by 115 runs. John Woodcock eulogised in *The Times*: 'Since the Second World War, no innings by an England captain has surpassed Gooch's. It stands out, not for artistic merit, but for skill and courage against a very formidable attack in awkward conditions at a crucial time.'

To quote Robin Marlar from the *Sunday Times*, 'Carrying his bat for 154 in a total of 252 puts Gooch on a pedestal above anything he or any of his contemporaries have done. Church bells have been run and sermons preached for less. At least we can put the man's name in lights. Which is more than Gooch himself will have been doing, and in that modesty he shares one of the principal characteristics of another England opening batsman, Jack Hobbs, The Master.'

Unfortunately, Gooch's 100th Test was a downer, a downright disaster. Everything went wrong for him and for England. It was against India in the first Test at Kolkata, which started on 29 January 1993. Gooch had started the tour in a depressed state of mind; he and his wife Brenda had separated. He suffered physically as well. The serious hand injuries he had incurred in the West Indies and Australia were now compounded by two debilitating bouts of illness in India. On the positive side, he had just completed his 100th first-class century and was looking forward to his 100th Test appearance. But on the eve of the Test he felt sick. 'Not only was I laid out in bed with the blinds drawn, I felt dizzy. I couldn't breathe properly and was continually throwing up,' he recalled. It was not easy for him to get up from the sick bed on the morning of the match but Gooch is made of sterner stuff.

He lost the toss but had India 3 down for 93. Just then India's captain Azharuddin resurrected his Test career by scoring 182 scintillating runs before he was caught by Gooch. Affected by the Kolkata smog, Gooch spent the whole time inhaling Vicks and applying it all over his face. 'I felt groggy right throughout the match. In retrospect I reckon I did really well to make 17 in the first innings and 18 in the second after I just lifted my foot and was out stumped. Most uncharacteristic. I just wasn't my normal self.' In reply to India's 371, England was forced to follow-on after managing only 163 runs, spinners Anil Kumble, Venkatapathy Raju and Rajesh Chauhan claiming three wickets each. Thanks to Gatting's 81, the visitors did better in the second innings but not well enough. India won by eight wickets. Neither Gooch nor his team-mates had any cause to celebrate as England lost the series 0-3. After four more Tests against Australia, he lost the captaincy of England as well.

Graham Gooch's career had its highs and lows but he always maintained his standard and the decorum. Tim de Lisle summed up his undulating career in the *Independent on Sunday*: 'His Test career has been a saga, a soap opera, a fifteen-year switchback ride, on and off the field; an unlikely mixture of success, failure, joy, heartbreak, acceptance, rejection, leadership, self-doubt and political intrigue on four continents. Every cricketer has his ups and downs; none has had quite such violent ones as this placid, modest, even-keeled man. Nobody has made more runs in a single Test match than Gooch, and nobody has made fewer.'

Rating for 100th Test: 1.5/10.

15 David Boon

Like Clive Lloyd, David Boon does not look like a cricketer. If you see them on the street, in the pool or signing autographs in everyday clothes, they appear anything but sports persons. Boon is made for comfort rather than for agility, you may observe. Short and stout, with a luxuriant moustache, he seems at first sight incapable of running 100 metres without huffing and puffing — let alone diving to take acrobatic catches. But dress him in flannel whites or Oz-yellow, put a helmet on his head and he becomes a pocket Atlas on whose shoulders rested Australian cricket from the mid-1980s to the mid-1990s.

Hyperbole? Statistics indicate that when Boon fired Australia ruled. When he flopped, Australia struggled. In 107 Tests, he scored 7422 runs at 43.66, hitting 21 centuries. Australia won 41 of these Tests, lost 25 and tied one, while 40 were drawn. In the 41 Tests Australia won, Boon averaged 53.03 with the bat, hitting nine centuries and 13 fifties. In the 25 Tests his country lost, his batting average was significantly lower, 23.45, and he registered only one century and eight fifties. Thus, it appears that there is a strong correlation between Boon's performance and Test results.

It would be too simplistic to state that Boon was the only player responsible for Aussie victories. There were bowlers (Craig McDermott, Shane Warne), wicket-keeper Ian Healy and batsmen — notably Allan Border, the Waugh twins, his opening partners Geoff Marsh and Mark Taylor, and of course Dean Jones … who also contributed richly. But no-one stands out as prominently as 'Boonie' in that period.

As Border wrote in the Foreword of Boon's autobiography, *Boon in The Firing Line* (1993), 'If you did a poll among world cricketers as to whom you would like to have out in the middle batting for your life, David Boon would rank very highly on the list.' Like Doug Walters, Boon epitomises a typical Australian. A tongue-in-cheek poster on who should become President should Australia become a Republic stated: 'Australia needs leadership from a figure who understands the essence of being Australian. There is only one man who fits this description — Boonie … The Queen is dead. Long live President Boonie.'

David Clarence Boon was born in Launceston, Tasmania, on 29 December 1960. His father Clarrie was a respected sports administrator and mother Lesley played hockey for Australia. At school, David excelled at cricket, Australian football and swimming. Lancashire coach Jack Simmons predicted that the 10-year-old lad would play for Australia and helped him on his way. A grateful David eventually named his son Jack after Simmons.

David made rapid progress, representing Tasmania at 17 and hitting the winning run in his first match. However, his transition from Sheffield Shield to Test cricket was not smooth and there were more snakes than ladders in his board game. Once there, however, he became a permanent fixture (except when dropped from the Sydney Test in 1987) and progressed to become an Aussie icon. Apart from his consistent batting as an opener or at no. 3, he was a magnificent fielder at short leg, snapping up catches from thin air. To some he appeared a robot in a helmet with extensible limbs.

I have been fortunate to witness many of David's controlled, stroke-filled but never spectacular innings on the Sydney Cricket Ground. His unbeaten 184 in the Bicentennial Test in early 1988 stands out. Australia trailed England by 211 runs and was forced to follow-on. A few quick wickets would have given England a victory, but rain and Boon stood in their way. Boon put on 162 runs for the opening wicket with Geoff Marsh (56) and remained not out till the end to ensure a draw. 'The Bicentennial Test has special memories for me,' Boon recalled recently to me. 'I was on my comeback trail, having been dropped in the previous Sydney Test in January 1987.' He grew in confidence in this, his sixth Test ton, facing 432 deliveries and hitting 14 fours; square cuts, cover-drives and pulls predominating.

His best series was in England in 1993. In 10 Test innings, he

Made for comfort, not speed. *(K.M.-H.)*

amassed 555 runs at 69.63, his best being an unbeaten 164 in the second Test at Lord's, his first Test ton in England. He had narrowly missed out in the first Test in Manchester, scoring 93, but then recorded centuries in the next three Tests. On the tour he totalled 1437 runs at 75.63 with nine centuries and topped aggregate and averages among the tourists.

The calendar year 1993 was memorable for Boonie as he scored 1241 Test runs; then second only to Bob Simpson among the Australians. A year earlier, the pavilion at the Launceston ground was renamed the David Boon Stand. He was only 31 then and in the middle of his Test career, a sure sign that he was close to being a cricket legend. Boon's highest Test score was against New Zealand in Perth in November 1989 when he scored 200 runs studded with 24 fours. It was a gem of an innings, full of thunderous off drives which made fielding at cover and mid-off a dangerous pastime. He looked always in command when engaged in century partnerships with tall Tom Moody and skipper Border. 'Getting a ball past Boon's bat was like trying to sneak a sunrise past a rooster' commented former New Zealand captain Jeremy Coney on the ABC radio. 'The tied Test in Madras in 1986 and our World Cup win in Calcutta the following year were special moments for me,' said Boon. 'The tied Test was fantastic.' Australia declared at 7 for 574 (Boon 122, a dehydrated but gutsy Dean Jones 210 and Border 106) and 5 for 170. India replied with 397, and when challenged to get 348 to win were all out for 347. It was only the second tie in Test history, the hero being off-spinner Greg Matthews who bagged 10 wickets in the match.

Boon also recalls with pleasure the two catches he took in his distinguished Test career. In the Melbourne Test of December 1994 against England, he latched on to an incredible catch at short leg to give Shane Warne a rare hat-trick. And in his 99th Test at St John's in the Caribbean he held a great catch off Steve Waugh to dismiss a brilliant Brian Lara for 88. 'It was most satisfying,' recalled Boonie, a master of understatement.

'Although I did not do very well in my hundredth Test, I have fond memories of that match. I consider it a great honour and privilege to play for Australia that long. For a milestone like representing your country 100 times is pretty special. Essentially, I treat any Test I play as an honour.'

To become only the second Australian — after Border — to wear the baggy green 100 times was an occasion he cherishes. His 100th Test was against the West Indies at Port-of-Spain in April 1995. Played on a green, bouncy, fiery pitch, the Windies skipper Richie Richardson had no hesitation in sending Australians in to bat. The pitch was damp as well and covered by grass nearly an inch long, a nightmare for batsmen facing quality speedsters Curtly Ambrose and Courtney Walsh. To quote Robert Craddock from *Wisden 1996*: 'Fast bowlers looked at it [the pitch] and grinned like fat men about to tackle Christmas dinner.' No team could total 140 in an innings and the first 30 wickets tumbled for 369 runs.

What a venue for a batsman to make his 100th Test appearance! Boon was fourth out at 37, scoring 18 out of Australia's total of 128. Only Steve Waugh made more, 65, which was the only fifty in the match. Ambrose was in his element, capturing 5 for 45. The match is remembered for the heated verbal on-field confrontation between Waugh and Ambrose. The bowler had to be tugged away by Richardson. 'It's Test cricket,' Waugh said later on.

Australia hit back, limiting the Windies to a narrow lead of eight runs as Glenn McGrath bowled with fire to grab 6 for 47. In the second innings, Boon failed again (as did nine other Aussie bats) as Australia collapsed for 105 and lost by nine wickets.

How did he feel playing his 100th Test? 'Pretty normal as far as I was concerned,' recalled Boon, as we watched a NSW *v.* South Australia Pura Cup match in November 2002. 'It was very nice of the West Indians to get together and applaud as I went in to bat. What a moment for me, representing my country in a Test 100 times! The Australian media made it a memorable event for me. Before the Test started, Mike Coward [of *The Australian*] and other journalists organised a team photograph with a plaque presented to me by the Australian Cricket Board. The ACB later presented me with an Australian cap framed with records and scores of my previous 99 Tests inscribed. As I said before it was a Test to remember for me, although I did not score many runs and Australia lost.'

Boon is a quiet person off the field and the fact that he opened up to a stranger like me suggests how highly he treasured wearing the baggy green cap. After each Aussie win he led the team choir singing the 'Under the Southern Cross' team song in the dressing room. He passed on his 'conductor's baton' to Ian Healy who relayed it to Ricky Ponting, another Tasmanian.

Allan Border, Boon's captain and an unashamed admirer, was moved to write, 'Man of all seasons and a quiet achiever, he never had a bad word for anyone. What a great bloke we have in the 5'2" Tasmanian with the flared pants! May there be more runs from the Keg on Legs.' He later remarked that Booney had a heart to match that of Phar Lap, the legendary Australian racehorse. You cannot pay an Australian sportsman a higher accolade.

Rating for 100th Test: 2.5/10.

16 Steve Waugh

Steve Waugh will go down in cricket history not only as among the most prolific run-getters and the most successful captain, but also as a motivator and a survivor. He prides himself in being physically fit — 'age is irrelevant' being his motto — but more importantly, he is mentally tough. Nothing was handed to him on a platter and he has had to struggle all the way, but the end line to his success story is: 'Whatever Steve wants, Steve gets — by hook or by pull.'

He somehow reminds me of a character from old comic books. To me he is 'Popeye, the Cricket Man,' 'Phantom of the Dressing Room' and 'The Road-Runner,' all rolled into one. I can visualise a scene where the vicious Wile E. Coyote ties him on the SCG batting strip and then lets a heavyweight roller run all over him until he flattens to a two-dimensional jelly. Then just as we bemoan the end of S.R. Waugh, he winks, throws his limbs out, gets 3-D, grabs a bat, thrashes Curtly 'Coyote' Ambrose off his back foot towards the cover boundary and starts running saying 'Beep, beep.'

Steve Waugh hardly shows emotion, neither on the field nor at press interviews where he answers questions truthfully, logically, but without drama. He is low key, yet he arouses passion, making a writer known for his bland statistics go in for flights of fancy. Waugh's epic century in the 2003 Sydney Test (which many wrongly thought was his swan song) brought tears of joy to the eyes of quite a few hardened journos. But Steve wondered what the fuss was all about. He is a professional cricketer, a top-order batsman, whose job it is to score runs.

Stephen Rodger Waugh, born in Sydney on 2 June 1965, is a legend but does not know it. A challenge brings the best out of him.

Doubt his credentials and he overachieves. As AAP journalist Doug Conway wrote in *The Waugh Twins*: 'The more pressure you put on Steve Waugh, the more he concentrates and bats all day. He becomes so completely engrossed in the mental struggles of cricket that there is no room for anything else, including the distraction of pain. It is as if his batting becomes a cocoon from the cares and woes of the world outside.'

There have been many memorable innings among his 30 Test tons. None more gritty and valiant than those in the Old Trafford, Manchester Test of 1997. Australia was in all sorts of trouble each time he went in to bat, being 3 for 42 and 3 for 39. He had painful injuries to both his hands in the later part of the first innings and throughout the second and an agonising abscess in the tooth. He was also burdened by the worry of a health scare concerning his infant daughter Rosalie which fortunately turned out to be a false alarm. Any mortal would have buckled under such pressure. Not Steve. He hung in for a total of over 10 hours and scored magnificent hundreds, watched by mother Beverley, wife Lynette and daughter Rosalie. More than his dual hundreds, what delighted Steve was that Australia won to level the series.

Greg Baum eulogised in the *Sydney Morning Herald*, 'To make one century in the face of hazardous batting conditions was brilliant enough. To make another while carrying a legacy from the first was special … Few batsmen in the world could have made [Steve] Waugh's first innings century, and he alone could have made another in the second innings, with his right hand so badly bruised from the battery of the first that he was still wearing a bandage on it the day after the match. It was the ultimate "Waugh wound."'

His performances made England's coach David Lloyd exclaim: 'Where can I get a Steve Waugh?' A British columnist suggested that ball bearings, and not blood, flowed through his defiant frame. Steve has been nicknamed 'Ice Man' and 'Tugga.' To me he is an 'Asbestos Man,' 'Rock of Gibraltar' and 'The boy who stood on the burning deck.'

Steve's biggest achievement was in the Caribbean in 1995 when he engineered a change of guard in world cricket supremacy. For 15 years and 29 Test series from 1980 onwards, West Indians were the undisputed kings of cricket with no second in sight. Their spectacular stroke-players (Lloyd, Richards, Greenidge, Haynes, Lara et al.) and the fiery pacemen Roberts, Holding, Garner, Marshall, Ambrose…) had not only defeated their opponents but pulverised them.

Twins who smile together win World Cup together. Mark (left) and Steve Waugh holding the 1999 World Cup at Lord's. *(Gift from Ken Hill)*

However, 3 May 1995 saw the changing of the guard at Sabina Park, Kingston. Australia, who had lost their last eight series to the Windies since 1978, suddenly staked claims as Test world champions by defeating them by an innings and regaining the Frank Worrell Trophy. The heroes of this remarkable turnaround were Steve and his twin Mark. In reply to the Windies total of 265, Australia amassed 531, thanks to an incandescent 231 runs added by the twins. Big Curtly Ambrose, with whom Steve had an on-field altercation in the previous Test, bowled only 11 overs that day and his partner-in-pace, Winston Benjamin, sat weeping during the drinks break and had to be cajoled to continue bowling — such was the heady domination of the Waughs from the Sydney suburb of Canterbury Bankstown. Steve went on to complete his maiden Test double century.

Robert Craddock wrote in *Wisden 1996*: 'He [Steve] was last out batting for close to ten hours and 425 balls, more than 150 short-pitched, and had 17 fours, one six and six aching bruises at the end of his greatest innings.' Trailing by 266 runs, the West Indies were bowled out for 213 and lost the Test, the series and their world-beaters image through one gigantic blow. In the series, Steve totalled 429 runs at the excellent average of 107.25.

Further triumphs awaited Steve in South Africa in 1997, where he scored 165 and added 385 winning runs with Greg Blewett (214) in the Johannesburg Test which Australia won by an innings. Steve was ranked as the best batsman in the world by the Coopers & Lybrand rating from 1995 until 1997 and in the top 10 for a decade.

Under Steve Waugh's captaincy Australia won 16 Tests in a row at the turn of the century. He has the best captaincy record in Test history, having won 36 of 49 Tests captained; a success rate of 73.47%. Don

Bradman comes next with 62.50% success rate, followed by England's Douglas Jardine and the West Indian Frank Worrell (60% each).

Steve's 100th Test was against South Africa on the SCG starting on 2 January 1998. Bungles and bloopers marked the start of this Test. Despite blazing sunlight the match started half an hour late as a pitch two strips away from the Test wicket was over-watered by an inexperienced member of the ground staff. The tenor Brian Giberston stopped midway through the South African national anthem, saying he could not hear the music properly and did not want to continue 'out of respect to the South Australian [*sic*] team.' There was also a car parking fiasco which prompted Sir Nicholas Shehadie, the former rugby international and now the chairman of SCG Trust, to groan: 'It's amateur hour.'

The batting on the first day of cricket also appeared amateurish as South Africa on winning the toss on a blameless pitch struggled to 5 for 197. With Shane Warne capturing 5 for 45, the visitors were bowled out for 287, skipper Hansie Cronje top-scoring with a painfully slow 88 in 335 minutes. Steve who was presented with a baggy green cap with all his Test statistics for his 100th Test on the opening day bowled eight economical overs, four of which were maidens and took 0 for 10. The following morning he caught tailender Paul Adams for nought, giving Warne his fifth wicket of the innings. The Waugh twins played superbly against some hostile fast bowling from Allan Donald. They counterattacked by adding 116 runs for the fourth wicket on the third day. At stumps on day-2, Australia was 3 for 174, Mark unbeaten on 78, Steve on 18, having added 71 runs that far. Facing Donald's fury in poor light was a challenge. As Mark recalls in *Mark Waugh: The Biography*, 'We were hit from pillar to post. Allan [Donald] was world class. Definitely the quickest white bowler in the world, probably as quick as anybody. He was bloody quick that day on a flat wicket. Some of the best bowling I've ever faced. Every ball was a test of your instincts.' No wonder the twins had ice-packs on their body in the dressing room.

Mark added another 22 the following morning before Shaun Pollock trapped him lbw for an even 100. The innings lasted 211 minutes and 186 deliveries and included 12 fours and a big six off Pat Symcox. Mark had thus celebrated his twin's 100th Test by scoring exactly 100. Will Steve get his century in his 100th? He seemed to be on target but when 85 he was bowled by Donald — to the agonising disappointment of his fans. He had battled for 279 minutes, faced

199 balls and smacked nine fours. He was hit four times by Donald and said that he 'loved it.' After the Test he told Simon Barnes of *The Times* (UK) how much he enjoyed facing fast bowling. 'It's the best thing about Test cricket. Having a quick bowler running at you, obviously giving his best. That's what it's all about and I really enjoy it.' His 85 in that match was much more valuable to him than 200 or so against ordinary trundlers. That, according to Barnes, was the 'Waugh Principle.' To me it was the road-runner's delight at thwarting the vicious coyote!

In the second innings the South Africans were dismissed for 113 as Australia won by an innings and 21 runs to lead 1-0 in the series. Warne took 6 for 34 for a match haul of 11 for 79, gaining his 300th Test scalp. It was a happy Test for the three Ws of Australian cricket.

Steve's record in limited-overs internationals as an all-rounder was also outstanding. His steady bowling 'at the death' won Australia many matches in the 1980s. His greatest achievement in LOI was winning the 1999 World Cup in England. It was his ice-cold temperament which made this possible, although his unbeaten 120 in the Super-6 round helped significantly.

The two matches against South Africa which enabled Australia to enter the semi-final and the final of the 1999 World Cup remain as among the most heart-pounding, hair-raising thrillers I have witnessed. Australia, under new captain Steve Waugh, outsmarted the opposition, psyching them into mental paralysis at the end. South Africa's opener, Herschelle Gibbs, was both the hero and the villain of the first South Africa *v.* Australia encounter at Leeds on 13 June. He scored 101 of his team's total of 7 for 271. Australia appeared in trouble at 3 for 48 when Steve entered. He was in superb touch and reached his 50 in 47 minutes. When 56, he offered a straightforward catch to Gibbs at mid-wicket. He 'caught' it and in excitement threw it up and away before controlling it and the umpire ruled not out. 'Ice-man' Steve allegedly mumbled something to Gibbs to the effect that he had just dropped the World Cup. This chance was morale-shattering for the Proteas. Give Steve one chance, one whiff and the opponents are finished. He added 126 runs with Ricky Ponting and remained unconquered with 120 when Australia reached the target with five wickets and two balls to spare. This victory took them to the semi-final where their opponents were once again South Africa.

Steve played mind games on the eve of the match, stressing the fragility and 'chockatibility' of the Proteas under pressure. With Shaun Pollock and Allan Donald bowling with fire, Australia was dismissed for 213 (Steve and Michael Bevan contributing 65 runs each). The match fluctuated bewilderingly. South Africa recovered from 4 to 61 through an 84 run stand between Jacques Kallis and Jonty Rhodes. After 44 overs it was sheer bedlam. Kallis was dropped in the deep, Pollock hit a six and a four before Shane Warne had Kallis caught by Steve. Then came Lance 'Zulu' Klusener, the Man of the 1999 World Cup. He attacked and brought his country close to victory. Steve did not panic. Damien Fleming bowled the final pulsating over. The scores were level with four balls to go and the last pair at the wicket. The in-form Klusener was on strike with only one run needed for a win in four deliveries. Surely they couldn't lose now. Everyone was tense except the Ice Man. There was a near run out during the third ball, panic and pandemonium. The next ball was a fuller delivery, Klusener hit and ran. Panic-stricken, Donald remained rooted to the crease watching the ball; both he and Klusener were at the bowler's end. Mark Waugh's backhand flick went to Fleming who rolled the ball to wicket-keeper Adam Gilchrist. Waking up as it seemed, Donald dropped his bat and scampered. Alas for him, too late. He was easily run out. It was musical comedy for the Aussies, but a tragic tuneless opera for the Proteas.

It ended in a tie but Australia entered the final because they had finished higher on the Super Six table. 'The best game of cricket I've ever played,' said Steve — showing emotions for once, the closest he came to saying 'beep, beep' to his mighty but temperamental opponents. Anything after this real life opera would be an anticlimax and the final against Pakistan at Lord's was just that. Australia lifted the World Cup by eight wickets with 29.5 overs in hand.

Steve continued performing solidly as batsman and captain in Test series at home and away, easily retaining the Ashes 4-1 in England in 2001. The 36-year-old Steve had scored 321 runs at 107.00, belting two centuries. His age had appeared irrelevant then. But when he had a poor home series against New Zealand and South Africa in 2001–02, he was suddenly labelled 'too old' — despite 90 run out against South Africa in the Melbourne Test. His form in the VB one-day series that season was equally disappointing and with the World Cup coming up in 2003, the selectors panicked and dropped Steve from the limited-overs squad to South Africa in 2002. This created a

Beverley Waugh flanked by sons Steve and Mark Waugh. *(Chris Passanah)*

national furore.

Steve was hurt, very hurt, but kept quiet. His double of 7000 runs and 200 wickets in LOIs was ignored. One bad season does not a winter make. In the past, great players like Greg Chappell and Mark Taylor had worse patches lasting longer. They were given opportunities to redeem themselves. They did, but there was no second chance for Steve Waugh in limited-overs internationals. One non-strike and he was out. Although he watched the 2003 World Cup only on television, he let his bat do the talking in domestic cricket. He scored prolifically in the ING Cup and the Pura Cup, leading New South Wales to a dual triumph. From the bottom, NSW had leapfrogged to the top in Pura Cup, thanks to his motivation, drive and confidence in young players.

There was much joy and celebration (except perhaps in the Caribbean) when Steve was appointed as captain for the tour to West Indies in April 2003. He is the most capped Test player with 160 Test appearances and the third player to score over 10,000 Test runs, after Gavaskar and Border. In 160 Tests (as at 15 May 2003) he has scored 10,265 runs at 49.83 with 30 centuries (highest score 200, significantly against the West Indies in 1995). He has also taken 91 wickets and 109 catches.

More than reaching personal milestones, he is a man on a mission. The last time he had led Australia to the Caribbean in 1999, the series was locked 2-all. He wanted to win the Frank Worrell Trophy in 2003 and did just that. Remember the ditty, 'Whatever Stephen wants, Stephen gets, beep-beep.'

Rating for 100th Test: 5.5/10.

17 Ian Healy

Ian Healy is recognised as among the best wicket-keeper batsmen in the game's history and first 'keeper to play 100 Tests. A veteran of 119 Tests, he holds the record of making most dismissals (395) including most catches (366) in Test history. His 29 stumpings are exceeded only by Australia's Bert Oldfield (an incredible 52 stumpings in 54 Tests), England's Godfrey Evans (46 in 91) and India's Syed Kirmani (38 in 88).

Healy also scored 4356 runs at 27.40 in Test matches, hitting four centuries, his unbeaten 161 against the West Indies in the Brisbane Test of November 1996 being his highest. He considers this Test as the highlight of his career. He went in to bat at 5 for 196 on a moist, swinging Gabba pitch when Michael Bevan was dismissed by Courtney Walsh for a first-ball duck. Calmly he added 142 runs with Steve Waugh and had valuable partnerships with the tailenders enabling Australia to reach 479. He had batted for six hours and hit 20 fours. He also made 45 not out from just 50 balls in the second innings. Thus, he had scored 206 runs in the match without getting dismissed and was adjudged Man of the Match.

'Apart from my strokes against the likes of Curtly [Ambrose] and Courtney [Walsh], my glovework was satisfying, we won the Test to go one up in the series,' recalled Healy during the 2003 Sydney Test against England when Steve Waugh, his partner of many summers, scored a stirring last ball century to equal Don Bradman's Australian record of 29 tons.

Healy has a mischievous look and a satisfied grin. He almost purrs as he talks; his eyes sparkle through his glasses, encouraging you to ask him provocative questions. One wonders how he could have ever sledged on the field, and he often indulged in mind games. As a batsman, he was in the same groove, if not the same class, as Ian Chappell. Both were compulsive hookers and were indefatigable in temperament. These days, the two Ians go hand-in-glove in Channel 9 TV boxes, intelligently analysing a game and dissecting a player's technique.

Ian Andrew Healy ('Heals' to friends) was born on 30 April 1964. His father, a bank manager, was a sports fanatic. As a boy, Healy was inspired by the wicket-keeping of Rod Marsh. In 1972, the family was moved to the town of Biloela, 600 km north of Brisbane. Young Ian was stimulated by the town's passion for all sports. He rode his bicycle to practice and play cricket, soccer, basketball, squash and rugby league. He became cricket captain at 11 and at a clinic conducted by Queensland wicket-keeper John Maclean he was allowed to examine his gloves. He still cherishes the memory.

Boy Healy played with adults, which perhaps explains his hard-headed approach to cricket. By the age of 17 he had developed that mental and physical toughness which typified his first-class and Test career. Despite solid performances with gloves and bat, he found it difficult to break into the Queensland Sheffield Shield team, as Peter Anderson was their regular 'keeper. Healy had played only six first-class matches when, out of the blue, he was selected for the tour of Pakistan in 1988. It was the most surprising selection since wrist-spinner John Watkins was picked in 1972–73 and off-spinner Peter Taylor in 1986–87. Many asked 'Healy, who?'

Healy was just as staggered at his selection. 'Was I being had?' he wondered. 'I phoned my parents and it was my father who actually confirmed the news.' Healy has national selector Greg Chappell to thank for this sudden promotion. Having played with Rod Marsh throughout his Test career, Greg was aware of the advantages offered by a wicket-keeper batsman. To him, Healy was ideally suited for the dual role. It turned out to be an inspired choice as 'Healy who' became a fixture of the Australian team for 12 summers, giving his unconditional support to captains Allan Border, Mark Taylor and Steve Waugh.

'Greg was impressed by Healy's tough temperament and efficient glove work,' remembers John Benaud. 'What I like most about Heals is the way he takes up a challenge with his opponents. A forceful

Ian Healy, smiling like a Cheshire cat. *(K.M.-H.)*

personality, he was a revivalist and the best in the world in the 1990s. More importantly, he kept so well to Shane Warne, who turns the ball square. Healy was up there with the best.' 'Bowwwwled Warnie' was the signature tune of Healy and echoed in all cricket grounds in Australia. Added Steve Rixon, former Test wicket-keeper and now the NSW coach, 'He [Healy] had his limitations earlier, but given the responsibility he became a topliner.'

Healy's most dramatic moment in his career was as a batsman. It came in the thrilling Port Elizabeth Test against South Africa in March 1997. After more than three days of twists and turns, it peaked to a climax. Australia needed five runs to win, South Africa two wickets. Amid cliff-hanging suspense, skipper Hansie Cronje came to bowl the final fateful over. Let Healy take over the narration: 'Mmm, well really, I didn't know what was going to come out. My legs were stiff, my adrenalin pumping and my nerves running everywhere. Well, the ball drifted down the leg and I thought I'd go after it. I got it sweet, really sweet.' It was a six, which won the Test. The Aussies had beaten the Proteas with what Healy recalls as a 'lottery shot.' He had become only the seventeenth batsman and the second Australian (after Alan Turner in 1976–77) to win a Test with a six.

Healy's 100th Test was also against South Africa and perhaps just as dramatic. There was a personal tragedy off the field and dropped catches, a major controversial decision and frayed tempers culminating in the visiting captain spearing a stump through the door of the umpires' room. It ended in a draw but no-one can call it dreary. It was the hotly debated Adelaide Test of early 1998. Healy's performance in this landmark Test was lacklustre, scoring 1 and 10, catching Herschelle Gibbs in the first innings and stumping him in the second.

Healy remembers this Test with affection and sadness. 'Many people, over 50 friends and relatives had specially come from Brisbane to Adelaide to support me in my 100th Test. But I was not quite focused throughout this Test. It was a sad period for me and the family as my father, Neville, had died a week before. I could concentrate when keeping wickets but not so much when batting. I played shots which I should not have as my mind kept drifting, thinking of Dad.'

For a long time Neville Healy coped with the chemotherapy well. However, just before Ian had to leave for Adelaide for the third and final Test, the family was summoned to the hospital where Neville had taken a turn for the worse. To quote Ian from his autobiography *Hands and Heals*, 'He [Dad] wasn't in much pain, but he couldn't speak and then Mum said something along the lines, "I'm sorry Ian, but I won't be able to come to Adelaide now." To be honest that was the last thing on my mind at that moment. Then I heard Dad give out a groan, as if he was trying to say something. And then he passed away ... It was very sad, the saddest I've ever been ... I'll always believe he heard Mum say she wasn't going to my 100th Test and decided that he wasn't going to let her miss it. I'm sure he was happy when he died, surrounded by his family who meant a world to him ... I owe my father so much.'

Ian Healy shared that poignant moment with me in the SCG press box during the January 2003 Sydney Test. 'I was a fraction distracted during that [1998 Adelaide] Test; having mixed emotions. I was very proud to represent my country 100 times but sad at Dad's passing. The Australian Cricket Board presented me with a handsome plaque in the shape of a baggy green cap with scores and statistics of all my previous 99 Tests inscribed. It was an emotional moment. Mum came to Adelaide for this Test, so did Uncle Phil, Dad's brother.

'I owe a lot to the South Australian Cricket Association for their hospitality in looking after my family and friends. The ground staff showed them around, offering drinks. The South African cricketers congratulated me warmly and offered sympathy for the personal loss. All Australian team-mates wore black bands.'

To the visitors' total of 517, Australia replied with 350, skipper Mark Taylor carrying his bat for 169 and Shaun Pollock capturing 7 for 87. Going for quick runs, South Africa declared at 6 for 193, Gary Kirsten 108 not out. Victory was in their grasp but a gutsy, unbeaten 115 from Mark Waugh and butter-finger fielding (in all 10 catches were floored) meant Australia salvaged a draw and won the series 1-0.

Ian remembers that his concentration drifted when batting, thinking about his dad. 'In the second innings when we were fighting to save the game and Mark Waugh was playing very well, I rushed out, hit two fours and then was caught behind playing at one I should have left alone.' Mark Waugh stayed right till the end, despite a controversial incident before day's end, when he accidentally knocked the bails off the stumps with his bat after being hit on the elbow. The video umpire, after watching the replays from all possible angles, declared him not out, much to the chagrin of the Safricans. Skipper Hansie Cronje was so livid that he later threw a stump at the umpire's door and was fined. 'Perhaps, Hansie did not do it but took the blame,' Healy suspects.

Thus ended Healy's 100th Test. 'I was proud of the achievement — especially as no other wicket-keeper had got there before,' he said. Had the game changed much from his 'Healy who?' debut to his 100th Test appearance a decade later? 'The game has changed at an astonishing speed,' he opines. 'The demands on the players' time on and off the field has ballooned. So has the money in the game, also the conditions in which the elite cricketers play has improved.'

How would one rank Healy as a wicket-keeper? Who better than his predecessor, the great Rod Marsh, to assess him? 'I've not seen a finer wicket-keeper — standing up to the stumps. He became an integral part of Australian cricket. His understanding of Shane Warne and Tim May behind the wickets had done a lot of good for their careers. He was an outstanding 'keeper, as good as any.'

Rating for 100th Test: 2/10.

18 Courtney Walsh

Courtney Walsh was the first cricketer and so far the only one to capture 500 Test wickets. He is also the first specialist bowler to play 100 Tests. He is the sort of player who makes you pen fractured proverbs: 'Nice guys finish first,' 'If at first you don't succeed, bounce, bounce again,' and 'What you lose in the swing, you gain in the reverse swing.'

It was almost impossible for a tyro quickie to break into the West Indian team in the 1980s, overcrowded with super-speedsters Michael Holding, Malcolm Marshall, Joel Garner ... Walsh was not the fastest in the Caribbean pace brigade, nor did he have Holding's grace, nor Marshall's swinging yorkers. He never got the new ball in his heyday, but like Old Man River he kept rolling along without fuss or self-pity, seldom losing his smile and never his cool. To quote Tim de Lisle from *Wisden Cricket Monthly* (April 1998), 'Never has one so quick come up so slowly through the ranks. For years Walsh was the pack horse of the great [pace] quartet, bowling long spells uphill and into the wind. It wasn't until his 59th Test, against Pakistan in May 1993, that he became Curtly Ambrose's regular partner.' In later years, the Courtney–Curtly combination gave batsmen little respite and many bruises.

Walsh's strength was bowling for long periods without losing line or venom. He changed his pace deceptively without any discernible change of action. As a result he hit more batsmen than his quicker contemporaries. It took him 12 Tests to achieve his first five-wicket haul in an innings. 'His gangling, slightly uncoordinated method of delivery suggested, treacherously, that the ball was coming in to the right-handed batsman,' observed former England Test cricketer Vic

Marks in *Wisden 2001*. 'This was not always the case and led to scores of victims in the slip cordon.'

Walsh was indefatigable. Once in stride nothing could stop him. He tore a hamstring during the 1997 Perth Test. The doctors proclaimed that he was unfit for this Test but after prolonged ice-treatment and vigorous stretching exercise, he bowled 20 overs and did not stop till the Test was won. Subsequently, he hobbled for two weeks but thought that a Windies win was worth the sacrifice. Like Australia's Glenn McGrath after him, Walsh targeted key batsmen, being an adherent of the dictum: 'Chop off the head and the rest will follow.'

Courtney Andrew Walsh was born on 30 October 1962. He made his first-class debut as a teenager, taking 15 Shell Shield wickets at 25.20 in 1981–82. He was chosen for the tour of England in 1984 but could not force his way into the Test team. However, he was selected in all five Tests in Australia and one in New Zealand in 1984–85, bagging 16 wickets. His difficulty in establishing himself as a regular Test cricketer made him moan, 'They want high pace all the time and that isn't my way. As a young bowler my idols were Michael Holding and Andy Roberts, who were both slowing up a bit when I started to play. They could bowl the odd quick ball still, but they varied it a lot. I admired the way they out-thought batsmen, with change of pace and length, and that's how I like to bowl.'

Tall, 197 cm (6'5"), and loose-limbed with a high arm, Walsh's action was more chest-on than a purist would prefer. His change of pace without change of action fooled many batsmen. He was also a marvellous team man. According to his Gloucestershire captain David Graveney, Walsh could diffuse potentially explosive situations with a humorous quip or some clowning. Walsh played for Gloucestershire and captured 203 wickets at under 19 runs apiece in 1985 and 1986. The highlight was his 9 for 72 haul against Somerset at Bristol in 1986.

Walsh took Test cricket's most prolonged hat-trick. In the Brisbane Test against Australia in November 1988 it took him two innings and 45 hours to complete one. The sequence started with Tony Dodemaide being caught by skipper Viv Richards off Walsh for 22. It was Richards' 100th catch in his 100th Test and Australia was dismissed for 167. The West Indies replied with 394 to lead by 227. Walsh was given the ball when Australia was 2 for 65. Mike Veletta

Courtney Walsh, the only player to capture 500 Test scalps, bowling like a well-oiled machine. *(Courtesy G.E. Features)*

pulled his first ball to mid-on and was caught by Carl Hooper for 10. His second ball found Graeme Wood, Veletta's brother-in-law, palpably lbw for a duck. Next man in was Australia's captain Allan Border, nursing a broken finger, and determined not to get out first ball to avoid a hat-trick. Belatedly, it dawned on the players and the spectators — aided by public announcement — that Walsh had already achieved the feat; his three victims in three balls being Dodemaide (two days previously), Veletta and Wood. It was the first Test hat-trick since 1976–77, the first in Australia since 1960-61 and the first to encompass two innings.

Like good wine Walsh kept improving as he matured. His best came when he was past 32 in 1995. He was awesome against New Zealand in the Wellington Test of February 1995 when he captured 7 for 37 and 6 for 18. This enabled his team to win by an innings and 322 runs, the fourth biggest victory in Test history and the heaviest defeat for the Kiwis. Surprisingly, it was a batsman friendly pitch. With bounce unobtainable, Walsh concentrated on immaculate line and length. His magnificent match figures of 13 for 55 was second best for a West Indian, after Holding's 14 for 149 in The Oval Test of 1976. Under Walsh's captaincy, the Windies won the 1995 Test series 1-0, their first series victory against New Zealand since 1955–56.

Walsh continued his outstanding form in the Antigua Test against Australia two months later. He bagged 6 or 54 and 3 for 92 and was adjudged Man of the drawn Test. 'Yet again, he [Walsh] was West Indies' get-out-of-jail card,' wrote Robert Craddock in *Wisden 1996*. Walsh has been engaged in three landmark Tests, his 100th in 1998 (which will be featured at the end), becoming Test cricket's highest wicket-taker in 2000 and reaching the magic, and thus far the unattained, milestone of 500 Test scalps in 2001.

The inaugural West Indies–Zimbabwe Test in March 2000 was memorable for Walsh as he overtook India's Kapil Dev's record of 434 Test wickets in the Kingston Test. Walsh fell prostrate and kissed his home turf when he had tailender Henry Olonga caught at short leg by Wavell Hinds for 2; the last wicket to fall and Walsh's 435th in his 114th Test spanning 16 seasons. He had overtaken Kapil Dev's record in 17 fewer Tests. Several thousand ecstatic fans lustily cheered the achievement of Jamaica's favourite son. The Windies won the next morning by 10 wickets to claim the historic series 2-0.

A year later, on 19 March 2001, Walsh, aged 38, reached a unique landmark in his 129th Test. In the Port-of-Spain Test against South Africa he climbed the unscaled mountain peak of 500 wickets. His 500th Test victim was South Africa's classy batsman Jacques Kallis, lbw for nought, a dubious decision. Walsh's team-mates formed a guard of honour as they filed off at tea. To honour him the West Indies Cricket Board presented him with a trophy.

Three years earlier, the 35-year-old war-horse had played his 100th Test in February–March 1998. He was the fifth West Indian (after Clive Lloyd, Viv Richards, Gordon Greenidge and Desmond Haynes) to join this club and the third after Steve Waugh and Ian Healy to do so in 1998. This was the fourth Test against England in Georgetown and the exciting series was level at one-all; the home team winning the second Test by three wickets and England the third Test — a thriller — also by three wickets.

West Indies batted first on an easy-paced wicket and scored 352, mainly through an enterprising 159 run stand between Shivnarine Chanderpaul (118) and Brian Lara (93). When Walsh came in to bat, he received a standing ovation, unusual for a no. 11 batsman. He remained unbeaten on 3. On a deteriorating pitch, England was dismissed for 170, Walsh had fine figures of 27-7-47-2. His victims were Alec Stewart caught by wicket-keeper David Williams for 20 and

Nasser Hussain lbw for 11. The Windies went for quick runs and were all out for 197, Walsh made a duck, nicking Robert Croft to 'keeper Robert Russell. Needing an imposing 380 to win on a difficult pitch, England had no answer to the dreaded combination of Ambrose, mean as ever, and the wily Walsh. They were shot out for 137, Walsh having impressive figures of 15-4-25-3. He trapped Mike Atherton lbw for 12, then had Hussain caught by Jimmy Adams for a duck and top-scorer Mark Ramprakash caught behind for 34. Tim de Lisle, the editor of *Wisden Cricket Monthly*, described the dismissal of Ramprakash by Walsh as the ball of the match, 'the juiciest of jaffas.' The Windies won by 242 to lead 2-1 in the series which made Walsh's 100th Test a happy one. He had taken five wickets in the match and had caught Angus Fraser off Carl Hooper for 2.

In 132 Tests, he captured 519 wickets at 24.45, taking five wickets in an innings 22 times and 10 wickets in a Test three times. Walsh was a rhythm bowler par excellence, mostly bowling within himself but suddenly producing something nasty, brutal and menacingly short. As a captain he was too mild to be effective. As a batsman he tended to be comical although he was associated in a century partnership with Hooper. Against Pakistan in the Antigua Test of May 1993, Hooper (178 not out) and Walsh (30 off 31 balls) added 106 runs in 103 minutes — a West Indies record for 10th wicket against all countries.

However, it is as a formidable bowler — not so much express as exquisite — and a gentleman cricketer that Walsh will be remembered. He kept playing until 2001 when he was 39 because his country needed him and he loved the game. In his later years, he was an ambassador for Jamaica and carries a diplomatic passport. He was and is universally liked as a bowler and a sportsman.

Rating for 100th Test: 5/10.

19 Mark Taylor

If someone were to invent a character as nice and uncomplicated as Mark 'Tubby' Taylor, critics would come down heavily on the novelist. 'No realism' would be their final comment. Taylor is more than just a Test cricketer. He has old-fashioned values. Like Colin Cowdrey and Courtney Walsh he gives lie to the theory 'Good blokes finish last.' Tubby is a good bloke who is universally loved and has reached the top or near top in everything he has attempted.

He was a left-handed opening batsman who could build a solid foundation and yet entertain. He pulled and drove balls for fours, cut and nudged for singles and accepted catches like a lizard catching flies. From a distance his mouth always seemed to move, not for sledging but for chewing gum. He led by example, winning 26 of the 50 Tests he captained. The only aspect he could not master as an active cricketer was the speed with which he spoke at pre- or post-match interviews. At times he sounded like a train going through a tunnel. One wondered with trepidation how he would sound when appointed as one of Channel 9's television commentators. However, with proper voice training and determination, he transformed himself into a capable expert broadcaster. If he had to discard chewing gum, so be it.

Mark Anthony Taylor was born on 27 October 1964 in a country town (Leeton) in New South Wales. The family moved to Wagga Wagga when he was eight. His hero then was Arthur Morris, another left-handed opening bat from NSW and one of Don Bradman's Invincibles on the 1948 tour. Forty-one years later (in 1989), Mark obliterated some of his records for which he received a letter of congratulations from Morris.

Taylor made a somewhat controversial Test debut, rather a non-

Test debut. For three hours he thought he was selected in the fifth and final Test against England in Sydney in January 1987 to replace an out of form opener David Boon. However, it was soon revealed that the inductee was his off-spinning club and State team-mate, Peter Taylor. If Mark was disappointed, he did not show it but continued scoring heavily for Northern Districts and NSW and made his Test debut two years later on the SCG against the West Indies. He was a victim of Curtly Ambrose in both innings and could muster only 25 and 3. His consolation was that Australia had vanquished the 'invincible' Windies by seven wickets thanks to Allan Border's amazing bowling spells of 7 and 46 and 4 for 50. This was Border's 101st Test and the figures astounded him as much as anyone else.

That year, 1989, was a marvellous one for Taylor. The tour to England was an outstanding success as he aggregated 1669 runs in 17 first-class matches at 57.55 which included 839 runs at 83.90 in the Tests. His run scoring was almost Bradmanesque in the Tests, compiling 136, 60, 62, 27, 43, 51, 85, 37 not out, 219, 71 and 48. When hitting 219 runs in the Trent Bridge, Notts, Test, he and Geoff Marsh batted throughout the first day, adding 301 and carried on the next day to make 329, the highest opening stand in an Ashes series.

Taylor's series aggregate of 839 runs had been bettered only by Bradman (974 in 1930) and England's Wally Hammond (905 in 1928–29) — both in five Tests, compared to Taylor's six. By the end of the year, with two more centuries against Sri Lanka in Australia, he became the first player to amass 1000 runs in his first calendar year of Test cricket, finishing 1989 with 1219 runs at 64.15 in 11 Tests.

This was a wonderful start of a career as he totalled 7525 runs at 43.50 in 104 Tests, notching 19 centuries, highest score an unbeaten 334, and 157 catches, a record since broken by namesake and fellow Australian Mark Waugh.

Taylor was at his best when the chips were down. He helped save the follow-on and defeats in two Tests I remember well. In the Sydney Test of January 1995, Australia was on her knees at 8 for 65 in reply to England's 309, but his 49 on a seamer's paradise when Darren Gough (6 for 49) was unplayable saved the day. England declared their second innings, setting the home team a daunting 449 to win. Taylor (113) and Michael Slater (103) put on 208 for the first wicket, going for a victory. But the middle order collapsed and Australia was lucky to draw the thriller.

Another Taylor masterpiece I recall was his captain's knock of 169 not out against South Africa in the exciting drawn Test in Adelaide in early 1998. He hit 21 fours and became only the ninth Australian to carry the bat and once again saved the follow-on against a rampaging Shaun Pollock who captured 7 for 87.

Between these two follow-on saving innings Taylor went through a bad patch when runs just dried up. It was almost embarrassing to watch a batsman as consistent as Taylor failing so frequently in his forgettable 1996–97 season. He made 153 runs at 17.00 in five Tests against the West Indies at home and 80 for 16.00 in three Tests against South Africa in South Africa. He had successive low Lotto-like scores of 7, 10, 11, 2, 1, 16, 8, 13, 38, 5 and 7 before he broke the drought with a defiant 129 in the second innings of the Birmingham Test against England in June 1997. Australia was facing a first innings deficit of 360 runs and he knew that another failure could mean the end of his international career. He had failed to reach a fifty in his previous 21 Test innings and he was castigated by every critic you could name. However, his 129 saved his career. He was still tentative around off-stump and followed this innings with low scores of 1, 2, 1 and 0 in subsequent Tests in England. Despite his poor form, he led inspiringly, beating the West Indies 3-2, South Africa 2-1 and England 3-2.

Mark Taylor returned to his imperious best in Pakistan in October 1998 when Australia won their first Test series in the subcontinent in 29 years. The tour is remembered for Taylor's epic innings of 334 not out in the drawn Peshawar Test. This equalled Don Bradman's record for a Test score by an Australian. On a flat, evenly grassed yellow pitch, Taylor played one of his best innings against some express bowling by young Shoaib Akhtar. He added 279 runs for the second wicket with Justin Langer and was unbeaten on 334, level with Bradman's score, at stumps on the second day. He had batted for 12 hours and hit 32 fours and a six to make the seventh highest score in Test history, the 15th triple ton and fifth by an Australian.

Cricket-lovers around the world waited for Taylor to get past Bradman's record and then go on to eclipse West Indian Brian Lara's Test record of 375 and become the first man to reach a Test quadruple century. But he declared the innings closed at the overnight score of 4 for 599. Many theories were put forward for this declaration. One explanation which quickly gained currency, although it was later denied by Taylor, was that he had refused to pass the record of the legendary Bradman. The real reason was that Taylor thought that a total of 599 was ample as he wanted to win the Test and the series.

Mark Taylor is now a relaxed cricket commentator. *(K.M.-H.)*

This self-sacrifice did not help as Pakistan amassed 9 for 580. Taylor made 92 in the second innings to aggregate 426 in the match, which remains second only to Graham Gooch's record of 456 runs (333 and 123) against India in the Lord's Test of 1990.

To Taylor, his 100th Test appearance was just as important as any of his Test centuries. This was against England on the Gabba in Brisbane in November 1998, the first Test of his final series. 'There was quite a build-up for my 100th Test and in a way I was keen to get the game under way,' he recalled. 'Before this Test started there was a presentation on the ground by Denis Rogers, the Chairman of the Australian Cricket Board. I was presented a baggy green cap in Perspex with scores of my previous 99 Tests etched on brass, recording every innings I had played. The national anthem was played and it was a moving moment for me. I still remember it fondly. I think I was more nervous than usual in the morning because I had won the toss and had to face the first ball. Once in the middle it was business as usual. In fact I was pleased when the pre-Test celebrations were over. The first over was traumatic though. Darren Gough bowled it and the ball hit my thigh pad. There was a loud appeal, negatived by the umpire. Soon I got off the mark which was a big relief.'

The Gabba had a curious look for this Test, with separate building sites cutting the spectator accommodation in two as new stands were being erected for soccer matches for the 2000 Olympics less than 10 months away. Taylor was perhaps thinking of a hundred in his 100th Test when opening bowler Dominic Cork had him caught by Nasser Hussain for 46. Australia was then in trouble, 4 down for 106, but was rescued by Steve Waugh (112) and Ian Healy (134) both being lucky as the butter-fingered Englishmen gave them two lives each.

With Glenn McGrath claiming 6 for 65 in a superb seam and swing exhibition, Australia gained a lead of 110 runs. 'I was not nervous in the second innings but dragged a ball from Cork back and was bowled without scoring. Wish I was nervous!' he joked. His partner Michael Slater caned all bowlers mercilessly to record his ninth Test ton in 172 minutes. Going for a victory, Taylor declared at 3 for 237, setting England 348 runs to win. The home team was on its winning way as England lost 6 for 179 but a spectacular thunderstorm at tea interval on the final day ruined Australia's chances.

Thus it was not a happy Test for Taylor but he proved himself an astute captain by winning the series 3-1. He equalled one and set one record during the series. He became the fourth captain (and third Australian) to 'coin wash' — meaning to win all five tosses in an Ashes series. The others were England's F.S. Jackson in 1905 and Australians Monty Noble in 1909 and Lindsay Hassett in 1953. Taylor set a record in the final Test in Sydney in January 1999. He equalled Border's record of 156 Test catches when he caught John Crawley for 44 in the first innings and went past it when he accepted Mark Ramprakash's nick in the second. Four weeks after this Test, Taylor announced his retirement from international cricket after captaining Australia in 50 Tests, winning 26 of these. He won 11 Test series out of 14. More than winning, he had brought dignity and respect back into what was now becoming a professional and commercial sport. The following year he was made Australian of the Year. On his retirement in early 1999, he received tributes from friends and foes. Here is a selection from his team-mates and opponents in the 100-Test Club:

Alec Stewart (England): 'The best captain I've played against or with. He's the most tactically astute, not afraid to try things out. He has a great cricketing sense.'

Wasim Akram (Pakistan): 'He was a great opening batsman, with all the shots. He was a very good tactician as a captain. He played positive cricket and always looked for a result in Tests.'

Shane Warne (Australia): 'It has been a pleasure playing under him. I would rate him alongside Ian Chappell, Richie Benaud and Allan Border as [one of] our greatest ever captains.'

Steve Waugh (Taylor's vice-captain and successor): 'Mark was a strong leader and he got the best out of his players. But at the same time he gave you room to be yourself and play your own way out in the field.'

Rating for 100th Test: 2.5/10.

20 Salim Malik

The 1990s witnessed bitter controversies and ugly upheavals in cricket — mostly involving bribery and match-fixing. These were not just allegations but in some instances were factually proven and recorded on tape. Many called this period cricket's saddest decade as reputations were tarnished and credibility lost. Illustrious names like Hansie Cronje and Mohammad Azharuddin, classical batsmen both and respected captains of South Africa and India, were banned from all forms of cricket at the turn of the century. Pakistan's captain, Salim Malik, among the first to be accused in this unsavoury episode, escaped the axe long enough to play his 100th Test. No such benefit of the doubt was accorded to Azharuddin, who had scored a century in his 99th Test before getting a life ban. Century today, oblivion tomorrow, so to speak.

Controversies and who-done-its aside, Salim Malik was a stylish batsman who scored 5768 runs at 43.70 in 103 Tests, hitting 15 centuries and accepted 65 catches. Among Pakistanis, he is the second highest run-getter after Javed Miandad (8832 runs at 52.57 in 124 Tests). Malik had strokes for every occasion and he played with a straight bat (on the cricket pitch, that is!). He was more orthodox in his technique than fellow prolific batsmen Miandad, Majid Khan and Zaheer Abbas.

Born on 16 April 1963, Malik was the son of a businessman. He started as a leg-spinner but club coach Raab Nawaz encouraged him to concentrate on his batting. When 16, he was selected for Pakistan's Under-19 team to India and Sri Lanka. He scored a century in his second first-class match. Still a teenager, he was picked to tour Australia in 1981–82 but did not play in a Test. He made his Test debut against Sri Lanka at Karachi in March 1982 and scored a century. At 18 years and 328 days, he had become the youngest to make a Test century on debut.

Malik showed his dogged streak against the West Indies in the Faisalabad Test of October 1986. The pitch was recently re-laid and was a minefield — a danger to life and limb. Pakistan was in strife at 5 for 37 and was being rescued by Salim Malik and Imran Khan when a lifting delivery from Courtney Walsh fractured the former's wrist. Pakistan was dismissed for 159 and the West Indies replied with 248. Pakistan lost their ninth wicket at 296, only 207 runs on. Bravely, Malik came in at no. 11, his left arm in plaster. He batted left-handed for one ball, then reverted to his normal right-handed stance, surviving 15 balls from quickies Walsh and Tony Gray in a courageous stand of 32 with Wasim Akram (66). He remained unbeaten with 3, as the home team made 328. Set 240 to win, the Windies collapsed for 53, their lowest ever Test score. Leg-spinner Abdul Qadir captured 6 for 16 in a mesmerising spell and Pakistan won by 168 runs.

'I have a short temper but I learnt to be patient in England [in 1987] and wait for the bad ball,' he recalled. He shone in England in the Tests at Headingley in Leeds and The Oval in London. He was unfortunate to be dismissed for 99 off the last ball of the day at Headingley. England batted first and were bundled out for 136. Malik batted with authority on the second day, his innings a lesson in sound technique and application, defending for five and a half hours for his 99 off 238 balls, hitting eight fours. With the score at 6 for 280, he drove a full toss from Phil Edmonds with a view to reaching his first century overseas but was caught by David Gower in the covers. He was devastated, a case of the nervous nineties. England collapsed for 199 to lose by an innings, Imran Khan taking 7 for 40, and a match haul of 10 for 76. The disappointment of his 99 was wiped out two Tests later at The Oval. Pakistan amassed a huge total of 708, Miandad hitting a spectacular 260, Imran 118 and Malik 102, his sixth century and the first outside Pakistan. He had added 234 runs with Miandad, a record for Pakistan's fourth wicket stand against England; his 102 came off 237 balls and included six fours. Forced to follow-on, England replied with 232 and faced an innings defeat but were rescued by Mike Gatting stroking an unbeaten 150.

When Australia, under Mark Taylor, toured Pakistan in late 1994, they found Pakistan captain Salim Malik a formidable opponent. In the three Test series he batted in all for 21 hours, scoring 557 runs at 92.83, beating Graham Yallop's Australia *v.* Pakistan's series record of 554 runs at 92.33 in 1983–84. In the Rawalpindi and Lahore Tests, Malik compiled match saving, series-saving centuries; 237 in Rawalpindi, 143 in Lahore. In a topsy-turvy first Test in Karachi, Australia was on top for four and a half days, yet lost by one wicket. Australia again started magnificently in the second Test in Rawalpindi, declaring at 9 for 521, Michael Slater slashing 110, Steve Waugh 98. But butter-fingered catching by the Aussies and Malik's superb resistance helped Pakistan to escape defeat. Pakistan was forced to follow-on and were facing a humiliating defeat when Malik played his highest and finest innings. Lucky to be dropped by Taylor at 20, he frustrated his opponents by scoring 237 in 443 minutes, his gallant innings studded with 34 exquisite fours. He was engaged in century partnerships with Aamir Sohail, Saeed Anwar and Aamer Malik. Just when Salim Malik appeared invincible, he fell to the hat-trick ball of debutant Damien Fleming.

To quote Fleming from *Hat-Tricks*: 'I shortened my run-up by about six metres and it had immediate effect as Aamer Malik on 65 had a whack at the ball and was caught by Michael Bevan. With the very next ball, I bowled a yorker and trapped quality batsman Inzamam-ul-Haq lbw. That dismissal marked the end of my over and then came drinks. I told "Billy" [McDermott] which proved prophetic, "Salim doesn't know it yet, but he's about to become a part of history."'

All the Australians knew about the possibility of a hat-trick but double-centurion Salim Malik was blissfully unaware. Tall Jo Angel bowled an over conceding nine runs. 'Then came my first ball of the next over,' remembers Fleming with relish. 'It moved away from Salim, he edged it and became Healy's fifth victim in the innings. Salim did not walk until the neutral umpire Karl Liebenberg lifted his finger. Initially there was stunned silence, then a burst of applause for Salim, for me and for cricket, I guess. It was one of the best balls I bowled, an inswinger. Big Jo Angel picked me up in air of jubilation, then spun me around which was a tremendous feeling.' But the match was drawn and Pakistan led 1-0 with the final Test in Lahore starting the following month. Salim Malik started in Lahore from where he had left off in Rawalpindi by scoring 75 and 143 to extricate Pakistan from disaster. In the second innings he was at his belligerent best, batting for over five hours and adding 196 runs in 215 minutes with Aamir Sohail (105) to dash Australia's hopes of a Test win. Malik was Man of the Match and Man of the Series for Pakistan.

The dark side of Salim Malik was brought out in the open a few months later. Australian players Shane Warne, Tim May and Mark Waugh alleged that he had offered Warne and May bribes to bowl badly in the thrilling Karachi Test. The Australian trio later made written statements to the International Cricket Council (ICC). Malik denied the accusations. As the ICC showed reluctance to act in 1995, the Pakistan Cricket Board (PCB) carried out its own inquiry conducted by Fakhruddin G. Ebrahim, a former Pakistani Supreme Court Judge and one-time Attorney-General. Ebrahim's investigations were further hampered by Australia's unwillingness to subject the three accusers to cross-examination in Pakistan, stating that they feared for their welfare. In view of this, Ebrahim concluded on 20 October 1995, 'The allegations against Salim Malik are not worthy of any credence and must be rejected as unfounded.' This judgment angered the ACB, especially when it was said that the allegations were 'concocted.' Warne, meanwhile, stuck to his story that he was offered $US200,000 by Malik on the fourth day of Karachi Test to bowl badly the following day. Warne refused, told roommate Tim May, captain Taylor, coach Bob Simpson and team manager Col Egar about the offer. Warne bowled at his best but Australia lost the cliff-hanging Karachi Test by one wicket.

Malik was replaced as captain in the next series and he was suspended pending further investigation. However, to the shock and dismay of the Australians he was selected to tour Australia as a batsman in 1995–96. The first Test in Brisbane in November 1995 appeared a soap opera as heavyweights Warne and Malik faced each other for the first time since the match-rigging accusation and denial. On the first day, Malik had made a splendid diving catch at mid-wicket to dismiss Taylor. Unfortunately, he needed six stitches in the split webbing on his left hand. To Warne's dismay, Malik would not bat as Pakistan was routed for 97. At his spanking best, Warne had bowled 16.1 menacing overs to grab 7 for 23. Forced to follow-on 366 runs behind, Malik went out to bat in the second innings at no. 8, his hand heavily bandaged, to sporadic abuse from the crowd. Warne dismissed him fourth ball for a duck, caught by McDermott at mid-off. This delighted Warne and as he wrote in *Shane Warne: My*

Autobiography: 'It shows there is justice in the game.'

Since then Malik has been in and out of the Pakistan team, the cloud of bribery and match-fixing hanging over his head. He was dropped after making a pair in his 99th Test (*v.* Australia in Karachi in October 1998) but returned for his 100th Test in the second Test against Zimbabwe at Lahore two months later. The newcomers to Test cricket, the Zimbabweans, had created shock waves by defeating Pakistan by seven wickets in the first Test in Peshawar. Panic-stricken, the Pakistan selectors made five changes for the next Test; starting with the captain Aamir Sohail. The official reason was that he was ill, but in fact he pulled out after clashing with coach Miandad and selectors Wasim Bari and Salamuddin Ahmed. Wicket-keeper Moin Khan was given the reign only an hour before the start of the match and Malik provided experience. Perhaps this could happen only in Pakistan. The weather gods appeared displeased at Malik's recall. There was dense fog on the first four days and the fifth day was completely obliterated. Zimbabwe batted first and made 183, fast bowler Waqar Younis took 4 for 54 and off-spinner Saqlain Mushtaq 5 for 32. Salim's sole contribution was catching Craig Wishart off Saqlain for 28. With Yousuf Youhana striking an unbeaten 120, Pakistan declared at 9 for 325. It may have been Malik's 100th Test but it certainly wasn't his day. In a mix up with Youhana, he was run out for 2 by a strong and accurate throw from Heath Streak. Malik had struggled for half an hour. The match was drawn due to heavy fog. 'Play Misty for Me,' headlined a tabloid. It was a most disappointing 100th Test for Salim Malik. 'I wanted to celebrate my 100th Test with a century, but unfortunately I got run out,' he said.

He played three more Tests against India in early 1999, totalling a modest 127 at 21.17 in them. This was the end for Salim Malik. The following year, nearly six years after allegedly offering bribes to Warne et al., he was finally given a life ban by the PCB on the recommendation of Justice Mohammad Malik Qayyum following a lengthy inquiry. One hopes posterity will remember Salim Malik more for his elegant batting, his 15 Test tons and his brilliant fielding at cover point with a pinpoint throw rather than for his off-field indiscretions.

Rating for 100th Test: 0.5/10.

21 Mark Waugh

Elegant and enigmatic, freakish and lazy, imperious and inimitable, immaculate and intriguing. Mark Waugh was all these and more. He was most of all an entertainer. Just as a Mozart symphony makes you forget your mundane worries, so does a Mark Waugh innings. No stress, no hassles. At times, you actually saw him yawn as he took guard. And just when you feared he would fall on the stumps half asleep, he would flick the quickest delivery from Curtly Ambrose or a doosra (mystery ball which spins the other way) from Saqlain Mushtaq to fine-leg for a four — his signature tune.

Mark Waugh had many signature tunes, a thundering cover-drive, a grass burning square-cut and an over-the-top on drive. As Pat Boone crooned in the 1950s on his girlfriend Bernadine:

Your separate parts are not unknown,
But the way you assemble them are all your own,
Oh, oh, oh Bernadine.

Mark had many nicknames too; 'Afghan' (forgotten Waugh, he made his Test debut five years after his twin Steve), 'Junior' (born four minutes after Steve) and 'Audi' (after his four ducks in a row in a Test series in Sri Lanka in 1992). He is his own man, is image conscious — about his hair and looks. He loves to punt and owns racehorses.

Among contemporary cricketers, only Greg Chappell, David Gower, Gundappa Viswanath and Mohammad Azharuddin had the same grace, that silken touch. Azharuddin eulogises, 'I just love watching Mark Waugh bat. I enjoy it even when he scores runs against us.' Apart from his classy batting and medium-pace to off-spin bowling, Mark was an outstanding all-round fielder. To quote Bob

Mark Waugh seems all set to top score against Sri Lanka in Colombo. *(Rowley Morris)*

Simpson, 'Mark is the best all-round fielder about. His catching in any position is brilliant and he has the safest pair of hands in cricket either in the slips or the outfield.' Mark Taylor, himself a brilliant slips fielder, agrees with Simpson's assessment.

I was fortunate to be present when an 18-year-old Mark Waugh (unknown except to his Bankstown team-mates) was presented the Richie Benaud Award for the Best Under-19 Cricketer in November 1984 in Sydney. Mark was then in Melbourne representing the NSW 2nd XI but I befriended his father Rodger and later his mother Beverley — the friendship has continued and ripened over two decades and was the genesis of my biographical *The Waugh Twins*.

My judgment might be coloured, but every innings I have seen of Mark Waugh — either live or on television, long or short — has given me a tingling sensation. It is almost impossible to select the best of Mark's masterpieces but one has to start somewhere and, appropriately, let's revisit his Test debut. Despite scoring almost 10,000 runs in first-class cricket and hitting 25 centuries, he could not break into an Australian Test team. Then suddenly he was included in the Adelaide Test of January 1991 against England at the expense of Steve. What followed in that Test was out of *Boy's Own* fiction. After waiting in the wings while his twin played 42 Tests, Mark achieved in his first Test what Steve did in his 27th. The confident debutant scored a magnificent century. Wrote John Thickenesse in *Wisden 1992*: 'He produced an innings which a batsman of any generation would have been overjoyed to play any time of his career, let alone in a first Test appearance and in a situation which verged on crisis.'

When Junior stepped in about an hour after lunch on the opening day, England's medium-pacer Phillip DeFreitas had sent back Allan Border and Dean Jones in four balls and the score was 4 for 104. It became 5 for 124 when a well-set David Boon was dismissed. Mark did not have time to be nervous. 'I had a close call first ball when I nearly got caught off the glove down leg side off Phil DeFreitas,' he recalls in *Mark Waugh: The Biography*. 'But after that everything fell into place. It was a lot easier than I thought ... I had no inhibition.' He stared with a Greg Chappell-like drive for three off his second ball. He reached his 50 in 74 balls and 100 in 126. With fours flowing from his bat, he hoisted 95 runs in the final session as partner Greg Matthews clapped and marvelled at the other end. Mark was dismissed the next day — Australia Day — for a bewitching 138, the 15th Australian and 54th player to notch a century in Test debut. 'It was an impressive first Test innings,' wrote Henry Blofeld in the *Weekend Australian*. Junior had made the art of batting incredibly easy.

Another of Mark's marvels was his century in the Birmingham Test in 1993. Australia started shakily, losing 4 for 80. Then Steve (59) and Mark (137) added 153 for the fifth wicket — the first century stand in Test cricket by a set of twins, and Mark's first Test ton on English soil. This was Mark at his brilliant and elegant best, picking balls off his toes and hitting wherever his fancy took him. His wristy, whiplash-like glances were a joy to behold as he dispatched 18 balls to the boundary like greased lightning.

Then came 1998 and he showed that he could defend when the chips were down. His match-saving innings in the Adelaide and Bangalore Tests indicated that he could be a rock as well as a gem-stone. In the third and final Test against South Africa in early 1998, he played his most controversial innings. South Africa piled on 517 and the home team replied with 350, skipper Mark Taylor carrying his bat for 169 as his name-sake Waugh continued his majestic form from the Sydney Test by stroking 63. The visitors declared their second innings at 6 for 193, challenging the Aussies to make 361 to win in 107 overs. At stumps on day 4 Australia was 2 for 32, Mark Waugh on 11, being lucky to be dropped by Adam Bacher off Pat Symcox when one. Continuing with his deadly form, Shaun Pollock (who had captured 7 for 87 in the first innings) attacked with gusto but his fielders let him down. Mark Waugh stood firm as he survived three chances when 96, 107 and 109. In a courageous display of self-denial one would expect from Border, Boon or Steve, Mark held up his end for 404 tense minutes. More importantly, he denied the visitors a victory and helped Australia claim the series 1-0.

The ending of this fascinating Test was shrouded in controversy by an incident in the final hour. As shown in myriad television replays, Pollock struck Mark above the elbow, the ball looping to Symcox at gully. The stroke was completed and no effort was made to take a run. In pain, Mark, who was on 107, walked away to nurse his arm and dislodged the bails with his bat. The on-field umpire referred the matter to the video umpire, Steve Davis. He took a long time and resolved the issue in Mark's favour. Skipper Hansie Cronje and his men were outraged by this decision. This is how Mark explained the weird occurrence: 'The ball hit me just above the elbow. I completed my shot and thought I was walking away. It must have hit a nerve in my arm because I could not control my arm. It went floppy and my bat hit the stump. I thought I had completed the shot, and after that it does not matter what happens.' Cronje, however, was not convinced. 'If somebody gets hit on the head, and he's a bit wobbly, and he walks on his stumps, he's out. That's all I want to stay.'

The same streak of self-denial coloured Mark Waugh's innings in the Bangalore Test against India in March 1998. Australia had lost the first two Tests by big margins and were determined to do better in the final Test in Bangalore. They regrouped and turned the tables by winning, thanks to the two Marks. There were many heroes for Australia, fast bowler Michael Kasprowicz taking 5 for 28, Michael Slater made 91 in the first innings and Taylor an unbeaten 102 in the second. The real hero, however, was Mark Waugh whose unbeaten 153 (13 fours and four sixes) enabled Australia to reach 400, only 24 behind India. It was his highest Test score. He was lucky too; when 37 he was 'bowled' by Venkatapathy Raju but the bails did not fall.

Call it the luck of the Waughs! In the second innings, he came out at 2 for 114 with 60 runs needed for victory and the hysterical local crowd screaming for an Indian win as the two Marks were surrounded by close-in fielders. However, the Marks enabled Australia to reach the target, playing no-frills cricket. This was Australia's first Test win in India since 1969, although the series was lost 1-2. In this Test Mark Waugh had amassed 186 runs without being dismissed, and he averaged 77 in the series. The elegance was still there but he demonstrated that he had some of Steve's steel as well.

Mark Waugh showed his versatility in limited-overs internationals. With Adam Gilchrist he formed a formidable opening partnership. Many players contributed to Australia's World Cup win in England in 1999, but the opening stands by Gilchrist and Waugh gave Australia flying starts. Mark took amazing catches too in this World Cup. He personally ranks the flying catch he took in the 1999 World Cup final at Lord's to dismiss Pakistan's W. Wasti as one of the three best he has taken. I vividly recall his flying through the air at mid-wicket to catch New Zealander Chris Cairns in the Perth Test of 1997–98. In fact, Mark holds the Test record of 181 catches.

He had a successful tour of England in 2001 when he scored 430 runs at 86.00 in five Tests, hitting two centuries and a fifty. His form slumped somewhat in the home series against New Zealand and South Africa in both the Test and VB limited-overs series in 2001–02. The selectors, in their wisdom, dropped both Steve and Mark Waugh from one-day internationals by March 2002. They were preparing for the 2003 World Cup by introducing new blood and the Waugh twins were suddenly considered too old. There was a national outcry when Mark was dropped from the Test series against England in October 2003. Disheartened, Mark announced his retirement from international cricket. The Australian media went berserk with the Mark Waugh news on the front, back and inside covers. It was like the assassination of a national leader, and to Waugh fans it was. His performances at Test, LOIs including World Cups and first-class levels have been staggering. How can one bad summer wipe out past deeds of valour?

In 128 Tests he scored 8029 runs at 41.82, with 20 centuries (highest score 153 not out), took 59 wickets at 41.17 and grabbed 181 catches — a Test record. Add to this his 8500 runs, 85 wickets and 108 catches in LOIs and 26,257 runs at 52.51 (including 81 centuries), 208 wickets and

Mark Waugh honoured by the Bankstown Mayor Kevin Hill after playing his 100th Test. *(Chris Passanah)*

441 catches in first-class cricket and you realise that Mark Waugh was more than a glancing glitter. He was truly great, apparently laid back but full of granite and gumption.

His 100th Test, against India in January 2000 on the SCG, was remarkable because it was the first Test match of the century and of the millennium. (Some may argue that the millennium started a year later.) At the initiative of skipper Steve Waugh, the Australians marked this new 'millennium' Test with a one-off appearance in caps of the style and shade of green worn in 1900. 'It sort of gave you a special feeling to be out there playing for Australia in the same cap guys wore a hundred years ago,' said Steve, who has a deep sense of history.

Mark Waugh holds the record for reaching the milestone of 100 Tests in shortest time, 8 years and 342 days since making his Test debut. Australia's Prime Minister John Howard presented Mark his 100th Test cap. Mark felt no different as he went out to field on 2 January. India's captain, the great Sachin Tendulkar, perhaps erred to bat first on a wet wicket, a seamer's paradise. The rain played hide and seek and India was bowled out for 150, Tendulkar providing lone resistance with 45 as Glenn McGrath took 5 for 48 and Brett Lee 4 for 39. Mark pouched two slips catches; makeshift opener Mannava Prasad for 5 off McGrath and Ajit Agarkar off Lee for a first-ball duck for the fourth time in succession.

Mark came in to bat at 2 for 49 to a huge reception from an excellent crowd of 38,705. He took only four balls to get off the mark with a trademark tuck behind square leg off spinner Anil Kumble. He went from 7 to 11 with his signature clip off the toes and did so again six runs later. He hit five fours and his home town supporters hoped that his fine touch was returning at the perfect time.

India's medium-pacer Javagal Srinath tried to stop Mark from scoring by bowling round the wicket and speared the ball into his hip region and above, with a short leg, leg gully, square leg and fine leg in wait for a catch on the on-side. Rather than get worried, Mark waited for the bowlers to spray on his legs or give him width outside the off-stump. He brought the house down by hitting a glorious drive off Agarkar. He received another rapturous ovation when he skied Kumble over mid-on for a six. With Justin Langer he added 97 runs for the third wicket. As Mark had hit a century in brother Steve's 100th Test on the same ground exactly two years previously, his home crowd hoped that he would get another ton in his own 100th. The answer was no, thanks partly to John Howard 'jinxing' him!

The Prime Minister, a self-admitted cricket tragic, filled a 40 minute guest commentator spot on ABC radio. Mark was full of confidence after that six off Kumble and in desperation skipper Sachin Tendulkar gave the ball to part-time bowler Sourav Ganguly. The first ball of the PM's commentary stint coincided with Mark Waugh's dismissal, to Mr Howard's barely disguised mortification. Mark was bowled by Ganguly for 32. He had in all batted for 102 minutes, faced 70 balls and hit five fours and a six. 'What can I say?' the PM told ABC listeners across Australia. Ganguly would have loved the Australian Prime Minister to commentate longer and more often! Mark received another standing ovation in recognition of the services rendered. Langer, who had played the worst innings of his career from 0 to 49, batted at his best from 50 to 223, adding 121 runs for the fourth wicket with Steve Waugh (57). Australia made a massive total of 5 for 552 before declaring and dismissed India for 261. India's stroke-player V.V.S. Laxman played a lone hand of 167 but Australia won by an innings and 141 runs and took the series 3-0. Mark accepted two more caches, Prasad for one and Ganguly for 25 — both off McGrath.

Remembers Mark in *Mark Waugh: The Biography*: 'Playing my hundredth Test was special. I was only the sixth Australian to do it [Border, Boon, Healy, Taylor and Steve were the others] so it was good to be up there with some of the greats. When you look at it, that's a lot of cricket. It means you've been a consistent player. You've obviously had highs and lows and learnt to cope with the pressures of Test match cricket. It's an achievement to be proud of... It's good to have been part of a winning team for most of that time. If I was like

Alec Stewart or Mike Atherton who have played a lot of Tests, but won very few, I don't think, I would have lasted as long.'

Adds brother Steve in his book, *Never Satisfied*: 'To play 100 Test not only proves that the cricketer has the skill to play the game, but is also an indication that he possesses the necessary mental toughness, physical durability and succeed regularly at the highest level. It also reflects the cricketer's love for the game ... Mark Waugh has deserved all the accolades that go with representing your country in 100 Test matches.' Wrote Allan Border in the Foreword of *Mark Waugh: The Biography*: 'It is no coincidence that Australia's success in the last ten years has coincided with the rise of Mark Waugh. How many other countries can boast one of the best one-day batsmen of all time, one of the best stroke-players of all time, a world record-breaking fielder who can turn a match in a split second and can be outstanding anywhere from the slips to the deep, a wicket-taking fast bowler, a wicket-taking slow bowler, a very competitive and aggressive player, someone who is rarely injured and a player with a knowledgeable cricket brain. You would have to look a long way to find a collection of cricketers with those abilities, but Mark Waugh has them all rolled into one.'

Rating for 100th Test: 3/10.

Back to school! The Waugh twins towering above the local junior singing choir. *(Chris Passanah)*

22 Michael Atherton

To see Michael Atherton in casual gear is a revelation. In the past I had seen him going out to bat (or field) in Test whites or one-day blues, at post-match interviews or in a tuxedo on formal occasions. There always was that worried look on his face, the furrowed brow, the distant haze. However, the Michael Atherton I met and interviewed in the SCG press box during the January 2003 Ashes Test appeared much younger. Gone was the anxious expression. It seemed as if an invisible iron had smoothed his brow. He looked boyish, barely out of teens and just out of school. And to think that he is almost 35 and a veteran of 115 Tests with 7728 runs and 16 centuries under his belt!

That's what retirement from competitive cricket has done to Michael Andrew Atherton, now a relaxed media personality with a spring in his step. He writes for England's *Sunday Telegraph* and *Wisden Cricket Monthly*, articulately commentates on radio and television and has time for cricket fans. His autobiography *Mike Atherton: Opening Up* has been reviewed favourably.

Born on 23 March 1968, Atherton showed promise as a cricketer at the age of nine. He made his first-class debut for a weak Cambridge University team in 1987. He went in at no. 3 but wickets kept falling at the other end and at one stage the score was a daunting 7 for 20. Atherton was not intimidated and scored an unbeaten 73 out of 135. In his fifth match, he made an undefeated 109 out of Cambridge University's 185 against Derbyshire. It was the first of his 54 first-class centuries and an innings he cherishes.

The exclusion of eight England players who rebelliously toured South Africa in 1989–90 under Mike Gatting enabled Atherton, 21, to make his Test debut. This was against Australia at Trent Bridge,

Nottingham. It was not a memorable one, far from it. He was out second ball for a duck. 'It bothered other people more than me,' he said. 'I hadn't suddenly become a bad player with one duck.' He made 47 in the second innings, but with low scores in the final Test he was excluded from the Caribbean tour.

His first Test hundred, 151, was against New Zealand at Trent Bridge in 1990 and he followed it up with another ton against India on his home ground, Old Trafford in Manchester. In the dual series, the 22-year-old had amassed 735 runs in six Tests at 66.81 with two centuries and six fifties. He had arrived, and for a decade he was either England's best batsman or very close to it.

As Matthew Engel wrote in *Wisden Cricket Monthly* (November 2002), 'Through 115 Tests, he never wavered, never wandered, never whimpered.' Although he went to an elite school and Cambridge University, he had that Aussie toughness and team-mates called him 'Iron Mike.' They admired his courage as a batsman and as a leader. To quote Engel: 'Had there been ten other cricketers in England between 1993 and 1998 with Atherton's ability and determination he would now be Sir Michael. But there were not. Instead of the regular helpings of adulation a successful captain expects, Atherton spent five years being insulted.'

It was nostalgic going down memory lane with 'Athers' during the 2003 Sydney Test, from the agony of his 99 run out at Lord's in June 1993, the 'dirt in the pocket' affair in July 1994 against South Africa at Lord's for which he was fined £2000 by Ray Illingworth, and the back injury that plagued him most of his career, to the ecstasy of his gallant centuries in Guyana in March 1994 and in Johannesburg in December 1995, his duels with 'white lightning' Allan Donald in July 1998, his highest career score of 268 not out for Lancashire *v.* Glamorgan in July 1999, his rather lacklustre 100th Test in Manchester in August 2000 and his retirement at 34 a year later.

I remember watching his 99 on television in 1993 as if it was yesterday. Trailing Australia by 427 runs, England was 1 for 173, Atherton on 97. He smacked an Allan Border delivery on the on-side. It was racing towards the boundary when Merv Hughes, less fat then, chased the ball and picked it up centimeters from the rope. At precisely that moment, Atherton turned and headed for the third run, which would give him his century. However, Mike Gatting, at the other end, spotted the danger and sent him back. Atherton slipped and hugged the pitch. Hughes' return was brilliantly picked by wicket-keeper Ian Healy and the stumps were broken, as was Atherton's spirit. If he was 17 or 87, he would not have contemplated a third run. John Thicknesse called it a 'moment of masochistic madness.' A year later in the Headingley, Leeds, Test against South Africa he again scored 99, one of the few unfortunate batsmen to register two Test 99s.

Atherton's name is linked with nail-biting nineties. After a dynamic duel with Donald at Trent Bridge in July 1998, he scored a marvellous unbeaten 98 to enable England to level the Test series. The Barmy Army has not quite forgiven Atherton for declaring England's second innings closed in the January 1995 Sydney Test at 2 for 255 with Graeme Hick unbeaten on 98. Nor probably has Hick!

Any regret about this declaration? 'To me my country always comes first, personal records afterwards. But for a pugnacious eighth wicket unbroken stand between Shane Warne and Tim May [which added 52 crucial runs lasting 77 minutes] England could well have won.' Spoken like a true 'Iron Mike'!

Career highlight(s)? 'Very proud to represent and captain England. There have been many moments to savour.'

My personal favourite is his marathon 185 not out in 643 minutes at Johannesburg in December 1995 to save the Test. Atherton was probably at his grittiest, he dropped an anchor and refused to budge. It was the fourth longest Test innings for England and according to Johnathan Agnew 'one of the most memorable Test innings ever played.'

Now to your 100th Test, Michael, at Manchester in August 2000 against the West Indies. 'It was a nice day, a sunny day, in front of my home crowd. The ECB Chairman, Lord MacLaurin, presented Alec [Stewart], also playing his 100th Test match, and me caps with 100 embossed on them. Also engraved decanters were presented to us. Although moved by this gesture, I was no more nervous than usual. I did not do too well in the drawn Test but Alec and Brian Lara hit magnificent hundreds. The ball spun a little bit. It was the third Test in the series which was locked 1-all. But we won the next two [Tests] convincingly to win the series 3-1 which was very satisfying.'

Atherton was dismissed in both innings by veteran speedster Courtney Walsh; caught at third slip by Sherwin Campbell for one and by wicket-keeper Ridley Jacobs for 28 as rain ended the match early.

Although his 100th Test was disappointing for him and his fans, the series had happy memories. Mike Atherton was adjudged Man of

Michael Atherton and Alec Stewart receiving commemorative caps for their 100th Tests. *(Getty Images)*

the Match in the final Test at the Oval after stroking 83 and 108. 'It was my first century against the West Indies in a long time [after five years], so the series had pleasant moments. If you can play for ten years at Test level, it means that in some way you have passed the test. It shows endurance, that you were good enough to stand up to what is a tough environment.'

A year later he retired from cricket and took up journalism. He appears to find match reporting and commentating less stressful than playing and captaining. Hence that boyish look in 2003. Atherton reminds Gideon Haigh of Len Hutton. 'He [Atherton] rationed his strokes while batting and rationed his words while captain ... He played so late yet the bat was always under close control, dropping down at the last moment, like a cat-flap closing.'

Summing up Atherton as stoic, Peter Roebuck drew a cameo picture of 'Athers' in *Wisden 2002*: 'Throughout the 1990s Michael Atherton was the face of English cricket. Head still, eyes wary, left elbow high and feet moving neatly into position, he dedicated himself to the task of scoring runs, resisting bowlers and protecting his team's position. For beneath his pale, youthful and sometimes defiantly stubbled exterior could be found a willful man blessed with skill and determination.'

Atherton's Lancashire and Test colleague, David Lloyd, was just as effusive. 'He was a player's champion who distanced himself from issues and people that he considered unimportant... He cared about England and about his players. Courage was arguably his greatest attribute. A fearless opening batsman, Atherton made us all feel proud to be British.'

Rating for 100th Test: 1.5/10.

23 Alec Stewart

Alec Stewart and Michael Atherton have been engaged in two rather unique events. They are the only cricketers to make their 100th Test appearance together. This was against the West Indies in Manchester in August 2000. Then in the Birmingham Ashes Test of July 2001, along with the Waugh twins — Steve and Mark — they provided the first instance of four centurion cricketers playing together. Stewart was successful in both these Tests, recording a century in his 100th Test in Manchester and top-scored in the first innings of the 2001 Birmingham Test. Born on 8 April 1963 in Merton, Surrey, Alec James Stewart is 40 at the time of writing, the oldest Test cricketer going around. And among the fittest and most versatile. He goes in to bat from numbers 1 to 7, keeps wickets and dives to intercept snicks like a man almost half his age. He also captained England with some success in the past.

He has cricket in the blood. His father, Micky Stewart, had played eight Tests for England, scoring 385 runs at 35.00 with two fifties (highest score 87) and accepting six catches. Later he became the manager of the England team about the same time Alec started his Test career. Being the manager's son was a cross young Alec had to bear. To quote Mike Selvey from *Wisden 1993*, 'It is a relationship that has always created debate. Nepotism, some have cried, has smoothed his progress. Nonsense, say others, if anyone has been held back it has been Alec because of Micky's need to be seen scrupulously fair to others.' Micky and Alec went out of their way to diffuse the whole issue, the father insisted that on a cricket field he had no son and referred to Alec as 'Stewie' while the son called his dad 'manager' —

even at home. Micky was there in Sabina Park, Kingston, Jamaica when 26-year-old Stewie made his Test debut in February 1990. 'My Test debut was the most memorable moment of my life,' Alec told me before the second VB Cup final in Melbourne in January 2003 where he scored a gutsy 60 but England lost by five runs. In his Test debut in 1990 he went in to bat at no. 3, scoring 13 in the first innings and was at the opposite end when England won by nine wickets. This was England's first victory over the West Indies since 1973–74 after a wait for 16 years and 24 Tests and their first win in Kingston since 1953–54.

Micky also saw Alec hit his first Test century (an unbeaten 113 against Sri Lanka at Lord's in 1991) but showed no emotion. 'He was absolutely delighted for me and he has told me so. But he was not going to show it publicly, in case he was misinterpreted,' said Alec. Now after over 7000 runs, 14 centuries and over 250 dismissals, even the sceptics realise that Alec is his own man. Always was, always will be.

Alec fondly remembers his twin hundreds in the Bridgetown Test in April 1994. On his 31st birthday, he opened the innings, scored 118 — his fifth Test ton — hitting 18 fours. Three days later he added another hundred (143 runs with 20 fours) to become the first England batsman to record centuries in both innings against the Windies and was made Man of the Match. What pleased him more was that his twin tons had enabled England to inflict only the second defeat on their hosts in 30 Bridgetown Tests. England became the first visiting team to succeed at Bridgetown since Bob Wyatt's England team in 1934–35.

Alec's other magic moment was in August 1998 when he led England to a victory against South Africa in the Headingley Test. Although he scored only 15 and 35, he took five vital catches as a wicket-keeper and led his country to a 2-1 series triumph. South Africa needed 219 to win but with fast bowler Darren Gough (6 for 42) in awesome form in front of his home crowd, the visitors lost by 23 runs. It was a thriller and the catches Alec took to dismiss rival captain Hansie Cronje for a duck, Brian McMillan for 54 and Alan Donald contributed to England's win. Alec also remembers the Melbourne Test of December 1998 which England narrowly and surprisingly won after he had scored 107 and 52.

However, the match closest to his heart is his 100th Test in

Manchester against the West Indies in August 2000. He was then in fine touch in the triangular one-day series, amassing 408 runs at 81.60. He scored 74 not out, 101, 100 not out (carrying the bat) and 97 in the Final. 'The ECB (England and Wales Cricket Board) chairman Lord MacLaurin presented commemorative caps with 100 embossed on them to Michael [Atherton] and me on the morning of our 100th Tests,' recalled Alec. 'We were also presented with engraved decanters.' Did he feel more nervous than usual as the Test commenced? 'Felt no different from any other Test. I played normally. We fielded on the opening rain-affected day.'

His chance to bat came on the second day, the Queen Mother's 100th birthday. The West Indies were dismissed for 157 on a damp pitch and England started poorly, losing 3 for 17 (including the other centurion, Atherton, for 1) when Alec walked in to bat. He settled in easily, and carrying his superb form in the one-day series he struck the ball square of the wicket with power and confidence. The pace of Curtly Ambrose and Courtney Walsh held no terrors for the 37-year-old warhorse who reached a glorious century in three hours and struck 13 crisp fours. At stumps he was unbeaten on 105, registering what the media called a 'regal century,' becoming only the fourth player to hit a hundred in his 100th Test. As he was still unbeaten at stumps, having added 179 precious runs for an unbroken fourth wicket with Test debutant Marcus Trescothick (65 not out), there was speculation that he would become the only cricketer to score 150 in his 100th Test appearance.

Unfortunately, he was dismissed second ball the next morning, caught behind off a smiling Ambrose. Walsh then removed Trescothick and England had lost both their overnight batsmen for two runs. Brian Lara, determined to outdo Alec, made 112 and the Windies declared at 7 for 438, setting England 293 runs in 71 overs before rain spoilt a run chase with England on 1 for 80. Alec was all padded up, perhaps dreaming of a second hundred, but was denied an opportunity. However, he had the satisfaction of keeping wickets satisfactorily and caught no. 3 batsman Wavell Hinds in both the innings.

The rain ruining a match that had the potential to be a thriller made the crowd feel cheated. Some of them lost their inhibition by streaking in varying degrees of nakedness. Alec Stewart will always remember 4 August 2000 when he joined all-time greats Colin Cowdrey, Javed Miandad and Gordon Greenidge to record a century

Alec Stewart acknowledges his century in his 100th Test. *(Getty Images)*

in his 100th Test. 'It was a special feeling, in a way more important than my other centuries — especially as England was in trouble when I walked in to bat. To play a hundred Tests shows one's ability and longevity in the game. It is an achievement you can be proud of.'

Rating for 100th Test: 7.5/10.

24 Wasim Akram

Taking into account both forms of international cricket — Tests and the one-dayers, Wasim Akram was arguably the best all-rounder. His record in the two versions of the game — especially in bowling — has been awe-inspiring. He has many onlys, firsts and mosts to his credit: the only one to take more than 500 wickets in limited-overs internationals (86 wickets ahead of his nearest rival), the only one to capture more than 50 wickets in World Cup, the only one to perform two hat-tricks in successive Tests, the first bowler (of two) to perform two hat-tricks in limited-overs internationals and the hitter of most sixes (12) in a Test innings.

Statistics aside, Wasim and his partner in pace, Waqar Younis, formed a lethal opening bowling partnership. They can be placed in the same class as Larwood and Voce; Lindwall and Miller; Trueman, Tyson and Statham; Hall, Gilchrist and Griffith; Lillee and Thomson; Roberts and Holding; Marshall and Garner; Ambrose and Walsh. Peter Roebuck was moved to write in the *Sydney Morning Herald* of 11 February 2003, '[Wasim] Akram is the most remarkable cricketer his country has produced and among the best the game has known…In Akram's hands a ball does not so much talk as sing. With a flick of the wrist and an arm that flashes past his ears like a thought through a child's brain he pushes the ball across the batsman and makes it dip back wickedly late, or bends it early whereupon it changes direction after landing.'

Born on 3 June 1966 to a moderately affluent middle-class family in Lahore, Wasim Akram was educated in a private school which encouraged sports. At 12 years he was opening the bowling and bating for the school, at 15 he was appointed captain. His life was consumed with cricket — at school, home, in the garage with his brother and on the streets with a tennis ball. At 18, his big inswing and powerful hitting attracted attention. Pakistan's former fast bowler Khan Mohammad taught him to lift his arm in the delivery stride which added to his speed.

He was lucky to be at the right place at the right time. He was practising in the Under-19 nets when who should pass by but Javed Miandad. The great Pakistan batsman was so impressed by Wasim's ability to move the ball at speed, while retaining control, that he insisted that the youngster be included in a squad of 14 for a three day Patron's XI mach against New Zealand at Rawalpindi in 1984–85. At Miandad's insistence, Wasim displaced the better known Tahir Naqqash in the final selection. Fewer first-class debuts have been more sensational than Wasim's: 7 for 50 and 2 for 54 as all around people asked, 'Who's this Wasim boy?' His victims included Test players John Wright (both innings), Bruce Edgar and John Reid (both innings). This is not the end of a fairy story, just the beginning.

Wasim went on to make his limited-overs international debut against the Kiwis at Faisalabad that season and was selected to tour New Zealand two months later. In his second Test in Dunedin in early 1985, the 18-year-old took 5 for 56 and 5 for 72. In 1987, he signed a lucrative six-year contract with Lancashire. His best match that summer was against Surrey when he captured 5 for 15 including a hat-trick and scored 98 runs off 78 balls.

He established himself as a Test all-rounder on the tour of Australia in 1989–90. In three Tests, he scored 197 runs at 39.40 with one match-saving century and took 17 wickets at 18.70 with three five-wicket hauls. He was made Man of the Match in the first two Tests and was undoubtedly the player of the tour with his brisk and varied left-arm bowling and belligerent left-hand batting. In the first Test in Melbourne in January 1990, he captured 11 wickets — 6 for 62 in the first innings and 5 for 98 in the second — but still could not stop Australia winning by 92 runs.

In a seesawing second Test in Adelaide, Pakistan almost lost the match, then almost won it thanks to a memorable 191 run partnership between Imran Khan (136) and Wasim Akram (123) for the sixth wicket. Trailing Australia by 84 runs, Pakistan lost 4 or 22 and was 5 for 90 when Wasim joined Imran. Wasim, not noted for his batting in a crisis, batted splendidly for 244 minutes and hit 18 fours and a six with tremendous power all round the Adelaide Oval. The fluctuating Test was drawn when Australia, needing 304 to win, was 6 for 233 at the close. It was Wasim's match as he had scored 52 runs off 89 balls in the first innings and captured 5 for 100 and 1 for 29. He won over the Aussie spectators with a match aggregate of 175 runs and six wickets and becoming only the third Pakistani after Mushtaq Mohammad and Imran Khan to score a century and take five wickets in an innings in the same Test.

After this tour, Wasim established himself as a top-class bowler but his batting was disappointing, although he did hit a century and a double century in a Test career embracing three decades. Wasim and Waqar Younis were enormously successful when Pakistan toured England in 1992. Wasim captured 82 wickets at 16.21 on the tour, the most by a visiting bowler since 1964. In four Tests he took 21 wickets at 22.00. 'It would be surprising if there has been a better left-arm bowler of pace; and he was the coolest of match winners with the bat at Lord's,' wrote Scyld Berry in *Wisden 1993*.

Wasim was adjudged Man of the Lord's Test after bagging 2 for 49 and 4 for 66 and scoring 24 and an unbeaten 45. Set 138 to win, Pakistan lost 8 for 95 when Wasim (45 not out) and tailender Waqar (20 not out) carried them to victory. Amid mounting tension, Wasim drove spinner Ian Salisbury through covers in the last over of the fourth day to win the thriller by two wickets. He continued with deadly spells in the drawn Manchester Test when he took 5 for 128 in the second innings, and 6 for 67 and 3 for 36 in the final Test at The Oval which Pakistan won by 10 wickets to secure the series 2-1. Wasim and Waqar were adjudged joint Men of the Series for Pakistan. There were some speculations about ball tampering after the series. England's manager and former Test cricketer, Micky Stewart, hinted that he knew how the Pakistani speedsters managed to swing the old ball more than the new one but was not prepared to say how.

Earlier, in 1990–91, Wasim became the third player after England's Maurice J.C. Allom (*v.* New Zealand, Christchurch, 1929–30) and Chris Old (*v.* Pakistan, Birmingham, 1978) to take four wickets in five balls. This was against the West Indies at Lahore. He was on a hat-trick after dismissing Jeff Dujon and Curtly Ambrose off successive balls in the second inning. He almost got a hat-trick when Ian Bishop edged the ball past Imran Khan who could not hang on to it. Off his next two deliveries he dismissed Malcolm Marshall and Courtney

Walsh. One near miss and he had missed the hat-trick twice in one over! He had to wait for eight years for his first hat-trick and then got his second in the next Test. In the Asian Test Championship held in 1998–99, Wasim performed hat-tricks against Sri Lanka in March 1999, at Lahore, and then at Dhaka. He became only the third bowler after Australia's Hugh Trumble and Jimmy Matthews to achieve two Test hat-tricks and the only to do so in consecutive Tests. Matthews performed two hat-tricks in the one Test and on the one day (28 May 1912), one in each innings against South Africa at Old Trafford.

Wasim was also the first player to take two hat-tricks in limited-overs internationals against West Indies and then against Australia, both at Sharjah in 1989–90. So far Saqlain Mushtaq is the only other cricketer to perform two LOI hat-tricks. Wasim also holds the record of hitting the most number of sixes in a Test innings. Against Zimbabwe at Shekhupura in 1996–97 he hit his highest Test score of 257 not out which included 12 sixes and 22 fours. He got past English great Wally Hammond's record of 10 sixes in his unbeaten 336 against New Zealand in the 1932–33 Auckland Test. Wasim's 257 off 363 balls in 490 minutes is the highest score by a no. 8 batsman in the Test arena. He came in to bat at 6 for 183 and took the score to 553, adding 313 exhilarating runs with Saqlain Mushtaq (79); a record for the eighth wicket.

Wasim Akram's 100th Test was against England at Faisalabad in November–December 2000. He was awarded a gold medal for competing in 100 Tests. Then it was business as usual. Pakistan won the toss and batted. With Yousuf Youhana scoring 77, they totalled 316. The most successful bowler was spinner Ashley Giles, who took five wickets including Wasim's. When only one, Wasim charged Giles trying to smash him out of the ground, but missed the turning ball and Alec Stewart stumped him. England replied with 342, a narrow lead of 26 runs, Graham Thorpe top-scoring with 79 before Wasim trapped him lbw. Wasim had bowled accurately but without much success, his figures being 26-6-69-1. Pakistan declared at 3 for 269, Abdur Razzaq at no. 3 making an unbeaten 100 on his 21st birthday. Wasim was not out on 4 when captain Moin Khan declared. England was set an achievable target of 244 in 62 overs but played for a draw. Perhaps their batsmen were deterred by poor umpiring. England's captain Nasser Hussain got bad decisions in both innings, first by

Wasim Akram showing the gold medal he received for his 100th Test to schoolchildren in Faisalabad, Pakistan. (Sportstar, *India)*

neutral umpire Steve Bucknor and then by home umpire Mian Aslam. Hussain did not show emotion but privately said that he was distraught. This perhaps increased demands for a third (video) umpire to be used for verdicts on lbws and catches. Wasim bowled only five overs and took 0 for 13; a disappointing 100th Test for him.

Lieutenant General Tauquir Zia, the Chairman of the Pakistan Cricket Board, said that he was not happy with the way the Pakistani team had performed and that it was only Wasim's past performances and his 'influential and strong position in the team' that had kept him in the squad. 'Just as important, it appears that captain Moin Khan wants him and that may be a crucial factor when the final XI comes to be chosen,' he added. In the third Test in Karachi, Waqar came into the side only 15 minutes before the toss after Wasim mysteriously withdrew with a reported back spasm. This surprised English columnist Ted Corbett. According to him, 'Wasim had bowled the most impressive medium pace spell in the first Test in Lahore and constantly troubled the England higher order batsmen in the second when he hit his old friend Mike Atherton on the helmet. He has consistently bowled with more enterprise and enthusiasm than Andrew Caddick, his opposite number in the England side.'

Wasim played four more Tests before retiring in May 2003. In 104 Tests he scored 2898 runs at 22.64 with three centuries (highest 257 not out). He also captured 414 wickets at 23.62, capturing five wickets in an innings 25 times and 10 wickets in a Test five times. His best bowling spell was 7 for 119 against New Zealand in 1993–94.

In LOIs, his record is just as impressive. In 356 matches he scored 3717 runs at 16.52 (highest score 86) and took a record 502 wickets at 23.52, bagging five wickets in an innings six times, the best being 5 for 15. He is the only one to grab more than 500 wickets, the next best being fellow-Pakistani Waqar Younis, 416 scalps at 23.84, followed by Sri Lanka's Muttiah Muralitharan, 325 wickets at 22.82. Wasim also leads in World Cup; being the only player to take more than 50 wickets. In 38 World Cup matches, he took 55 wickets at 23.83; the next best being Australia's Glenn McGrath, 45 wickets at 20.77 in 28 matches.

A complex character requires a perceptive writer to sum him up. So over to you, Peter Roebuck: '[Wasim] Akram's cricket has been not so much a career as a merry-go-round. Along the way he has dazzled many batsmen, taken hundreds of wickets, helped his team win a World Cup [in 1992], captained his country a few times, refused to talk to his successor and been implicated in several scandals, always protesting his innocence with the air of a cat appalled at claims he was responsible for devouring a nearby fish … A compelling figure, he has the grin of a playboy, the face of a gangster and the powers of a cricketing genius.'

Rating for 100th Test: 2/10.

25 Shane Warne

One can write volumes on Shane Warne and yet leave yawning gaps. A champion wrist-spinner, he is a master of his art. *Wisden 2000* ranked him as the no. 4 Cricketer of the Century — behind legendary Don Bradman, Garry Sobers and Jack Hobbs and above Viv Richards and Dennis Lillee. The next best spinner was Bill O'Reilly, ranked at no. 15.

Warne is an extraordinary character, a sensation about to happen. As an outstanding spinner, he was both a shock and stock bowler, both penetrating and containing. Indian batsmen will scoff at this assessment as they have always attacked him with gusto. The fact remains that as soon as a captain hands the ball to Warne a hush descends upon the ground. There is an air of expectancy as he removes his cap, gives it to the umpire and twirls the ball. What will he bowl — a leggie, a googly, a flipper or an arm ball? Face it, Warne is a legend and the most controversial figure in the game's history. He makes headlines practically every week, and not for performances on the field only. An extrovert, he tends to put his foot in the mouth and in some way he is his own worst enemy.

He has been questioned over allegations of bribery (for providing weather and pitch information to an illegal bookmaker), and involved in a cigarette scandal (caught smoking when publicly telling others to quit the habit), a sex scandal in England which perhaps cost him the Australian captaincy and the 'drug' scandal for which he received a 12 month ban starting in February 2003. At one stage he was nicknamed 'Hollywood,' apparently for his vanity. So conscious he is over his appearance that he put his brilliant Test career on hold to get rid of his double chin. Or so we are told!

Shane Keith Warne was born in Melbourne on 13 September 1969. He wanted to be an Australian Rules footballer but was not selected. This has been cricket's biggest gain. He has bleached blond hair and fondness for fast food and beer. He was 97 kg when he made his Test debut against India in the Sydney Test of January 1992 as an inexperienced 22-year-old. He had then played only four Sheffield Shield matches but had impressed the selectors with the way he spun the ball.

Indian batsmen enjoy facing spin bowling and Warne's Test debut was forgettable. He took 1 for 150 as India piled on 483 runs, Ravi Shastri hitting 206 and teenage wonder Sachin Tendulkar 148. Warne regrets dropping Shastri when he was 66 but eventually dismissed him 140 runs later. The podgy leg-spinner went wicketless in the next Test in Adelaide and was dropped before the final Test in Perth. Who would have thought then that within a decade this Test discard would become a superstar with his on-field brilliance and off-field dramas?

After the halting start, he was invited by Rod Marsh to return to the Australian Cricket Academy and was coached and encouraged by former Test leg-spinner Terry Jenner. Apart from coaching, Jenner advised him on dietary and beer restrictions. Soon Warne was taking wickets, starting in the Colombo Test against Sri Lanka in August 1992. In the first innings he had unflattering figures of 0 for 107 as Sri Lanka amassed 547 and led Australia by 291 runs. Set a mere 181 runs to win, the home team was marching towards victory at 2 for 127. To Warne's surprise, skipper Allan Border brought him into the attack. He responded to the trust shown in him by taking 3 for 11, in one magical spell 3 for 0. Off-spinner Greg Matthews chipped in with 4 for 76 and incredibly Australia won by 16 runs. What a turnaround!

With his confidence restored, Warne showed his wizardry in the Melbourne Test against the West Indies in December 1992. He captured 7 for 52 in the second innings and Australia won by 139 runs. To beat the Windies in the early 1990s was a huge achievement and heralded the arrival of Warne as a quality spinner. He also triggered a renaissance in the art of spin bowling — especially in limited-overs cricket. Warne remains very grateful to Border for the faith he showed in him. Then came the tour to England in 1993 and that 'ball from hell.'

This was Warne's first ball in Test cricket on English soil, in the Old Trafford, Manchester, Test of June 1993. It was bowled to Mike Gatting, an acknowledged master of playing spin. Warne flicked the ball vigorously out of the back of his hand. It set off on the line of Gatting's pads and then dipped in the air further towards leg side until it was about 45 cm (18 inches) adrift of the stumps. Then the ball bounced, turned and fizzed across Gatting's body to clip the off bail. Gatting remained rooted at the crease for several seconds in disbelief

Shane Warne, the Sultan of spin. *(Getty Images)*

and returned to the pavilion in a trance. Warne took 4 for 51 and 4 or 86. In the six-Test series, he pouched 34 wickets at 25.79. And the legend grew.

One can go on extolling his performances, his hat-trick against England in the Melbourne Test of December 1994, his 300th Test scalp, his getting past Kapil Dev's previous record of 434 wickets. Only injuries and free-scoring Indian batsmen plagued his Test career in the past. Now, the 12 month ban imposed on him in February 2003 for taking a banned substance has delayed him from overtaking Courtney Walsh's Test record of 519 wickets. At the time of writing, he is only 28 wickets short of the record.

Warne's most satisfying Test was against Pakistan in Brisbane in November 1995. He had magnificent match figures of 11 for 77 (7 for 23 and 4 for 54). To dismiss Salim Malik for a duck in the second innings delighted him. Warne explains in *Shane Warne: My Autobiography*: 'Motivation is something I never lack at any time, but especially not against a team such as Pakistan, and when they came to Australia in 1995–96, I was fully pumped up. Only a year had passed since Salim Malik attempted to bribe Tim May and myself to bowl wide of off stump in a Test match. Worse still, a couple of weeks or so before the series was due to begin, the judge in Pakistan leading the first investigation had decided that Malik was not guilty, effectively branding us liars. So I desperately wanted to beat Pakistan to set the record straight and show there was some justice in the game.' Sure enough, Australia beat Pakistan and Warney finished with his second best figures of 11 for 77. But what did it have to say about who was lying? All it proved was that Warne is a great bowler — which even his worst critics know. Drama is Warne's forte, not logic!

Warne considers Tendulkar as the best batsman he has bowled to. Among bowlers he has three favourites, Merv Hughes for his big heart, Curtly Ambrose and Glenn McGrath. His best ball? To him it was not the ball that confused, confounded and bowled Gatting. It was the ball that dismissed West Indian Shivnarine Chanderpaul in the Sydney Test of 1996. 'It was the biggest turning leg-break I've bowled to take a wicket and the best ball I've bowled,' he told Malcolm Conn of *The Australian*.

Warne became the seventh Australian, fifth bowler and first spinner to play 100 Tests. This was against South Africa in Cape Town in March 2002. And what a memorable Test it turned out to be — in my opinion the best 100th Test to date. Sixteen of his family members and closest friends had flown to Cape Town for this landmark match. They included his wife Simone, parents Keith and Brigitte, and his mates from Australia and Hampshire. South Africa won the toss and started poorly. Shortly after lunch they were 6 for 92, but the tail wagged and they totalled 239. Warne had figures of

28-10-70-2; his victims being Neil McKenzie bowled for 20 and Makhaya Ntini caught by Mark Waugh for 14. Warne also caught Paul Adams off Jason Gillespie for 35.

Australia struggled and were 6 for 185 when Warne joined Adam Gilchrist. They added 132 quick runs before Warne was caught by Jacques Kallis off Paul Adams for a hurricane 63 in 65 balls. He had batted for only 102 minutes and hit a six and 10 fours. Gilchrist was equally aggressive and his unbeaten 138 took Australia to 382, a lead of 143 runs. South Africa fought back gallantly, McKenzie being unlucky to be run out for 99. Warne bowled with skill and variety to capture 6 for 161 in 70 marathon overs (15 of them maidens). He had dismissed four top order batsmen, Herschelle Gibbs for 39, Graeme Smith for 68, Kallis for 73 and Ashwell Prince for 20. He also dismissed tailenders Ntini for 11 and Dewald Pretorius for nought. For the first (and so far, the only) time a cricketer had taken 6 wickets in an innings and 8 in the match when playing his 100th Test. Before him Kapil Dev had the best figures of 4 for 69 in an innings and 7 for 151 in his 100th Test 13 years previously.

A victory target of 331 was not easy on a worn pitch but Matthew Hayden (96) and Justin Langer (58) gave Australia a heady start of 102. Then Hayden and Ricky Ponting added 99 for the second wicket. Australia was cruising at 2 for 251 but lost the next four wickets cheaply. At 6 for 305, Warne joined Ponting and scored 15 unbeaten runs. Ponting reached his century and won the Test with a six. The visitors took an unbeatable 2-0 lead to claim the Test match championship title. Warne's happiness was complete when adjudged Man of the Match for his all-round excellence. During this match, he had become only the fourth cricketer after New Zealander Richard Hadlee, India's Kapil Dev and Pakistan's Wasim Akram to reach the Test double of 2000 runs and 400 wickets.

With due apologies to Colin Cowdrey, Javed Miandad, Gordon Greenidge and Alec Stewart, I would rank Warne's performance in his 100th Test as the greatest ever. He had scored 75 runs in the match for once out and had bowled 98 magnificent overs (25 maidens) to capture 8 for 231.

'There are few fairy tales; this is as close as it gets,' he said after the Test. 'The way it has panned out — to win the Test, the series and the Championship Trophy. It's been a fantastic Test match and one I'll always remember.' Then he added prophetically, 'Nothing lasts forever so that emphasises the point that you have to enjoy yourself because you never know when it's over.'

Rating for 100th Test: 9/10.

26 Sachin Tendulkar

What can one write about Sachin Tendulkar that the cricket world does not already know? The sign of greatness is when opponents praise you. And when Australian opponents shower praise on you, you are a legend. Steve Waugh, not known to give an inch to a rival, recently said, 'You take Don Bradman away and Tendulkar is the next up, I reckon.' To most Indians, it is: 'You take Mahatma Gandhi away and Sachin is next up.'

Bishan Bedi, the former Indian spinner and captain, described Tendulkar as 'the greatest Indian alive.' To cricket-mad Indians, he is a god, no less! There are many religions and gods in India, which divide her people. However, Tendulkar is one god who unites. As his biographer Gulu Ezekiel says in *Sachin*, 'In a country of a billion plus where the "unity in diversity" mantra of the state machinery has begun to ring hollow, Tendulkar has emerged as perhaps the nation's unifying force.'

C.P. Surendran writes in *An Anthologist Among the Marxists and Other Essays* (edited by Ramchandra Guha), 'Every time he [Tendulkar] walks to the wicket, a whole nation, tatters and all, marches with him to the battle arena. A pauper people pleading for relief, remission from the life-long anxiety of being Indian … seeking a moment's liberation from their India-bondage through the exhilarating grace of one accidental bat.' In mass popularity, Tendulkar outglitzes even the Bollywood stars. And it's just not Indians who go all ga-ga over Sachin magic. Peter Roebuck, a balanced hard-nosed columnist, places Tendulkar in divine category after the 2003 World Cup. His 98 off 75 balls against arch-rival Pakistan at Centurion in South Africa inspired him to write in the

Sydney Morning Herald: 'His breathtaking assault on a furious Pakistan attack brought thousands to their feet; waving, chanting and roaring themselves hoarse. Tendulkar was blistering and monumental, ruthlessly attacking off both feet and on both sides of the wicket.' Roebuck went on to describe the short, stocky Indian icon as 'the greatest player and the best batsman to appear since the war.'

Was this going over the top? Since World War II we have witnessed outstanding batsmen in Hutton and Compton, Harvey and the Chappells, Worrell, Walcott and Weekes, Viv and Barry Richards, May and Cowdrey, Sobers and Kanhai, Graeme Pollock and Zaheer Abbas, Gavaskar and Border, Gower and Miandad, the Mohammads, Lara and the Waughs … What perhaps puts Tendulkar in a class of his own is his all-out domination from the first ball faced, brilliant stroke-play off good length balls, intense concentration, superb timing and an air of invincibility. Add to these his impeccable manners and off-field humility. Despite millions of dollars earned, he has remained a man of the people who loves the game. His era coincided with major upheavals — corruption and bribery, sledging and umpire-abuse — but he has been universally respected, his reputation untarnished.

It was his domineering stroke-play (backed up by fine seam bowling and solid batting support from Rahul Dravid, skipper Sourav Ganguly, Mohammad Kaif and Yuvraj Singh) that led India to the World Cup final in Johannesburg in March 2003. They lost tamely to a vastly superior Australian side, but Tendulkar was adjudged Man of the 2003 World Cup. He had outscored the next best batsman by almost 200 runs in amassing 673 runs at 61.18 with a century and two memorable nineties. It was an occasion to cherish for him when the legendary Garry Sobers presented him with a golden bat after the final. It was his fourth World Cup since 1992 and he has accumulated 1732 runs at 59.72. The next best is Javed Miandad with 1083 runs at 43.32 in six World cups.

Despite his superstar status, Tendulkar has maintained a dignified mature outlook and protects his privacy. When he married Dr Anjali Mehta in 1995, he rejected massive sums of money from satellite television for live coverage. His father, a university professor, had imparted a sense of perspective and work ethic.

Sachin Ramesh Tendulkar was born in Mumbai on 24 April 1973. He was a child prodigy, breaking records from the age of 12 when he scored a century for his Sharadashram School. When barely 14, he amassed unbeaten scores of 207, 329 and 346 in the space of five innings, one of them contributing to an unbeaten partnership of 664 with Vinod Kambli (also a future Test cricketer), a record in any form of cricket. He was coached by Das Shivalkar and Ramakant Achrekar and his role models were Sunil Gavaskar and Viv Richards.

Tendulkar made his Test debut aged 16 years and 205 days, the youngest from India and the fourth youngest ever. It was a baptism of fire against Pakistan's pace trio of Imran Khan, Wasim Akram and Waqar Younis at Karachi in November 1989. By a coincidence, this was Kapil Dev's 100th Test. Coming in at 4 for 41, Sachin made 15. In the series he scored 215 runs at 35.83 with two fifties. Thus it was a promising rather than a spectacular start.

The following year he toured England and hit his first Test century at Old Trafford, Manchester, in August 1990. He was then only 17 years and 112 days, the second youngest after Pakistan's Mushtaq Mohammad to hit a Test ton. He took a long time to get off the mark in the first innings and scored 68 runs. Set 408 runs to win in a minimum of 88 overs, India made 6 for 343, helped by Tendulkar's unbeaten 119 off 171 balls in 224 minutes; adding 160 runs with Manoj Prabhakar (67 not out). The match was drawn but it proclaimed the arrival of a master batsman.

Noted Anglo-Australian writer and historian, David Frith, headlined his story in *Wisden Cricket Monthly*: 'Hail the Boy King.' He wrote: 'How could anyone so young be so good at the highest level? He was wearing Sunil Gavaskar's off-white fibreglass pads, which made him appear to waddle rather like one of television's cuddly toys… Tendulkar dealt with everything England dished out, driving powerfully and cutting like a flash.' After Tendulkar received Man of the Match award, Richie Benaud was moved to say on TV: 'We'll see a lot more centuries from his bat. I hope I'll be around to see them.' Manager Bishan Bedi was perhaps misquoted in the British press as saying, 'Every English woman would like to seduce Sachin.' This created an uproar as he was only 17 then. Bedi later clarified to Sachin's biographer Ezekiel, 'I meant *mother* him, not seduce him!'

Then followed his tour of Australia in 1991–92 and his memorable Test hundreds in Sydney and Perth. In Sydney in January 1992, his 148 came off 216 balls in five hours and included 14 fours. He had added 196 runs for the sixth wicket with Ravi Shastri (206) as India totalled 483 runs (Shane Warne making an inauspicious Test debut with a 1 for 150 whacking). Leading by 170 runs, India had Australia on the ropes but bad weather helped the home side avoid defeat, being 8 for 173 at the end. At 18 years and 256 days, Sachin had surpassed the previous record held by Australia's left-hand great batsman Neil Harvey who was 19 years and 121 days old when scoring his century in 1947–48. Harvey witnessed Sachin's Sydney masterpiece and eulogised, 'He is the best player I've seen since ages. I love the way he places the ball past fieldsmen and his backfoot technique is superb.'

On a bouncier pitch at WACA in Perth the following month, Sachin hit a captivating 114 out of India's moderate total of 272. His second fifty came off only 55 deliveries. In all, he hit 16 fours, the bulk of them from square cuts. His batsmanship made ABC commentator Tim Lane gush, 'This boy is from heaven. He will do anything.' Allan Border said, 'If he could play like this at 19, I shudder to think what he will be at 25.' What indeed! Seven of his centuries were scored before he reached 21, and 31 tons before he reached 30, unique records. Having gone past Don Bradman's feat of scoring 29 Test tons at Headingley in August 2002, he is all set to break fellow Indian, and hero, Gavaskar's world record of 34 Test hundreds. In fact Gavaskar has warned Sachin that he will not be forgiven if he did not get 50 Test centuries!

As at 15 May 2003, Tendulkar has scored 8811 runs at 57.59 in 105 Tests, hitting 31 centuries (highest score 217 against New Zealand at Ahmedabad in 1999–2000), and accepting 68 catches. Among batsmen playing 100 or more Tests, his batting average of 57.59 is the highest, Javed Miandad coming next with 52.57.

Tendulkar's statistics in limited-overs internationals are just as staggering. He normally opens the batting to put the bowlers on the back foot. In 314 matches he has aggregated 12,219 runs at 44.43 with a strike rate of 86.54. He has hit 34 centuries (highest score 186 not out *v.* New Zealand at Hyderabad in 1999–2000) and 62 fifties, and has taken 97 catches. No-one else has reached even 10,000 runs in LOIs, India's Mohammad Azharuddin being next best with 9378 runs at 36.92 in 334 matches.

It is beyond the scope of this publication to describe each of his masterpieces at Test and LOI levels. He has reserved his best for playing against Australia in India. He was at his diabolical best in the

A Stand at the Wankhede Stadium was named after Sachin Tendulkar at the start of the Mumbai Test in 2002, his 101st. BCCI Chief Jagmohan Dalmiya is on his left. *(Santosh Harhare/*Mid-Day, *India)*

1997–98 series when in three Tests he scored 446 runs at a massive average of 111.50 with 155 not out in Chennai and 177 in Bangalore. No wonder the Australian bowlers get ecstatic when they see the back of Sachin Tendulkar. At 29 years he became the youngest cricketer to play his 100th Test, the only under-30 centurion. It would have been ideal if Sachin's landmark Test was staged in Mumbai, his birthplace. Gavaskar made an impassioned plea to Jagmohan Dalmiya, the president of the Board of Control for Cricket in India (BCCI) to ensure that Sachin's landmark Test should be staged in his home town. But that could not be arranged and his 100th Test was played at The Oval in London, the fourth and final Test against England in September 2002. The series was locked one-all and Sachin's fans were fantasizing a super performance. Will he become the first player to score a 150 in his 100th Test? (So far the highest has been Gordon Greenidge's 149 in 1989–90).

Sachin's 100th was more an occasion for India than for him. Political heavyweights from his state Maharashtra flew in just to be there and bask in his reflected glory. The media made it into a mega event and according to the *Independent on Sunday* Sachin 'could not breathe without being quoted.' At the start of the Test, he spoke about the 'very, very high expectations' that he always had to live up to but conceded that 'life would be boring' without them. Before the toss, he was presented with a silver salver by the team and when he came out to bat he received a thunderous standing ovation. It was a high scoring match and both the teams, it seemed, went for a draw. England won the toss and batted and batted to total 515, mainly through Michael Vaughan's 196. Not to be outdone, India replied with 508, Dravid scoring a monumental 217. When Tendulkar reached his 50, he received more than usual cheers. Will he bat on to reach 100 ... and perhaps even 150? He did not. When he had made 54 runs (with 10 crisp fours) in 114 minutes off 89 balls on the third day, he was hit on the base of his pad by a full toss from Andrew Caddick and adjudged lbw. He had added 91 runs with Dravid. There was no second innings and the match meandered towards a yawning draw.

Recalls Peter Roebuck in an e-mail, 'I remember Sachin's 100th Test because a century was expected but he was like a cat on a hot tin roof and did not settle. His dismissal was not a surprise. He hates a fuss and dislikes matches being about him. These occasions tell us something about the men involved.'

His 101st Test was played at Wankhede Stadium in Mumbai in October 2002. Coincidentally, it was West Indies captain Carl Hooper's 100th Test. Both were felicitated by the BCCI. To honour Sachin a section of the North Stand of the Wankhede Stadium was named Sachin Tendulkar Stand. The felicitation was on the same scale of the one extended to Gavaskar when he completed 34 Test centuries and to Anil Kumble for taking all 10 wickets in a Test innings. The soft-spoken, unspoilt Sachin appeared more embarrassed than jubilant at the compliments heaped on him.

Tendulkar is more than just a successful sportsman. In April 2002, *Time* (Asia) magazine chose him as one of their Asian heroes for the second time in three years. Inside, 'The Bat out of Heaven' shared space with freedom fighters, human rights activists and other luminaries.

Tendulkar has received glowing praise from the mightiest on the land to the most humble. The tribute he treasures is the one by Don Bradman. In an interview by Ray Martin on Australia's Channel 9 in May 1996, Sir Donald said, 'Sachin plays more like me than any other modern player I've seen.'

Rating for 100th Test: 4/10.

27 Carl Hooper

Test cricket was 91 years and four months old when Colin Cowdrey became the first cricketer to play 100 Tests. This was in Test match number 639. Carl Hooper, the last centurion at the time of writing, took only one month and one Test to join Sachin Tendulkar in the 100 Tests Club. He became the third player to enlist in this exclusive group in 2002, to join all-time greats Shane Warne and Sachin Tendulkar.

Although not as illustrious as the other two, Hooper holds two records. He is the only cricketer to play 100 matches, score over 5000 runs and take more than 100 wickets and 100 catches in *both* Tests and limited-overs internationals. Also, on the negative side he is the only 100-Test player who has *not* been made *Wisden*'s Cricketer of the Year — triviologists please note!

A graceful but inconsistent batsman, Hooper has been described as an 'enigmatic stylist' and a 'batting beauty queen.' In an interrupted Test career spanning 17 summers from 1987 until present time, he has promised much but achieved less than predicted. 'When Carl came into the West Indies team, he was a quiet, shy person but an immensely talented batsman,' recalls former colleague Winston Davis. 'People say he hasn't fulfilled his potential but too much was expected of him.'

To tag an up-and-coming cricketer as the second Don Bradman or Viv Richards is often a curse. When Hooper burst into the Test arena he was seen by many as the next Richards. Another former Test player, Ron Headley, commented that Hooper was the closest thing he had seen to Lawrence Rowe, a West Indian batsman who scored 214 and 100 not out in his Test debut in 1971–72 but did not reach his full potential. Hooper, however, was too individualistic to be a second Richards or a third Rowe. He was his own man, he dazzled and dwindled, then sizzled and fizzled. A graceful batsman against both pace and spin, he appears in full flow before unexpectedly losing his wicket. He tended to lose concentration, perhaps lacking the willpower to convert fifties into big scores. He was more laid back than 'never-say-die,' more like David Gower than Steve Waugh. Hooper was also a genuine off-spinner with an easy languid action and an alert slip fielder.

Carl Llewellyn Hooper was born in Georgetown, Guyana, on 15 December 1966. He made 37 in his Test debut in Mumbai against India in December 1987. But it was in the next Test in Kolkata that he impressed critics with a finely chiselled unbeaten 100. He added 169 runs with Gus Logie (101) for the fifth wicket and 73 with Jeff Dujon for the unbroken sixth. At 21 years and 12 days, he became the third youngest West Indian after George Headley and 'Collie' Smith to score a Test ton. So elegant was Hooper's stroke-play that 'cognoscenti sat back in anticipation of further artistic canvases,' to quote Christopher Martin-Jenkins in *World Cricketers*. They had to wait for four more years, however, before he performed something equally breath-taking.

Hooper's progress was hindered by back problems, a lack of fixed batting order (captains sending him to bat at no. 3 to no. 6) and form swings. However, the selectors' persistence was rewarded in the December 1990 Lahore Test against Pakistan. It was crisis time as the West Indies were on the verge of surrendering their first Test series to any country in nearly a decade. The pitch was slow and kept low but Hooper batted with confidence alongside a debutant Brian Lara against the feared pace trio of Imran Khan, Wasim Akram and Waqar Younis. The Windies were 3 for 37 when Hooper joined Lara and the two 'stylish enigmas' added 95. Then he added 61 in 56 minutes with Malcolm Marshall and reached his century in 242 minutes with eight fours and a six. This saved the Test and the series.

Hooper topped first-class averages on the tour to England in 1991, amassing 1282 runs at 85.46, hitting four centuries including 111 in the Lord's Test with 14 fours and a six. He was at his spectacular best in the final Test at The Oval. Trailing England by 243 runs, the Windies were forced to follow-on. In the second innings, Hooper produced a stupendous cameo on the fourth morning, striking three sixes — two off leg-spinner Phil Tufnell (who had caused havoc in the first innings with a 6 for 25 haul). Hooper made a quick-fire 54, a magnificent display of stroke-making.

Against Pakistan in Antigua in May 1993, Hooper played an innings of poetic majesty after initial luck against Waqar Younis' in-swingers. His unbeaten 178 off 247 balls in under five hours contained every stroke in the book (and some which were not, to regain the strike). He belted four sixes and 19 fours in a firework display and 106 runs with last man in, Courtney Walsh. It was a West Indies Test record for the 10th wicket. Hooper also played for Kent in County Cricket and his best was an unbeaten 236 against Glamorgan in 1993. The mid to late 1990s saw Carl losing interest in playing for the West Indies. It was sad to see a cricketer as talented as himself play in Melbourne as a club cricketer. But he bounced back and took over the West Indies captaincy from Jimmy Adams after they were whitewashed 0-5 in Australia in 2000–01.

We witnessed a positive Carl Hooper against the touring Indians in 2002, reaching heights he had promised but seldom achieved. He scored centuries in three out of five Tests and led his country to an unexpected 2-1 series win. His only Test double century came in his home Test at Bourda in Georgetown, Guyana. The skipper steadied the ship after the Windies were 3 for 44 in the first Test, Lara out for a duck. Full of concentration and rock solid, he added 113 with Ramnaresh Sarwan (53) and 293 with Shivnarine Chanderpaul (140). The Windies totalled 501, India replied with 7 for 395 and the match was drawn. India won the second Test at Port-of-Spain, Trinidad. However, Hooper turned the tables on India by making 115 in the third Test in Barbados as the Windies levelled the series. Then he scored 136 in the fourth Test in Antigua. The West Indies won the fifth and final Test in Jamaica and the rubber 2-1. In the series, he had amassed 579 runs at 82.71. Wrote Harsha Bhogle in *Wisden Cricket Monthly*: 'The fairy tale journey from an unsettled club player in Melbourne to a resurgent international cricketer is now complete. Relaxed in his mind and settled in his faith, Hooper is at last ready to put the right numbers alongside his unquestioned ability. It is a wonderful story for it tells that life never shuts its doors on you.'

Much was expected from the West Indies and Hooper when they toured India in late 2002. But they had not reckoned on India's phenomenal home record and the slogan, 'Tigers at home, mice

Carl Hooper, an enigmatic stylist, is a ferocious hooker. *(Getty Images)*

overseas.' The first Test of the series in Mumbai in October 2002 was Hooper's 100th and his 20th as captain. He became the third player after Allan Border and Javed Miandad to play his first and 100th Tests on the same ground, Border on MCG, Miandad in Lahore.

It was a Test to forget for Hooper. He failed in both innings: c. Sanjay Bangar b. Zaheer Khan 23; c. & b. Harbhajan Singh for one. He bowled 11.5 overs including three maidens and took one for 40 — his sole victim being tailender Javagal Srinath, caught behind for 31 — and took Anil Kumble's catch. To add to Hooper's woes, the Windies lost the Test by an innings. Although it was his 100th Test, the limelight was focussed on Sachin Tendulkar playing his 101st on his home turf. Both were presented with plaques for their durability and achievements from BCCI president, Mr Jagmohan Dalmiya while a section of North Stand in the Wankhede Stadium in Mumbai was named the Sachin Tendulkar Stand. The Windies lost the three-Test series 0-2, which made the normally understated Hooper blunt at the post-match conference where he said his team 'just did not play cricket.'

Hooper lost his captaincy to Brian Lara after the West Indies failed to reach the Super-6 (second round) of the 2003 World Cup in Southern Africa. This was disappointing for Hooper as his later years had been his finest — especially in the Caribbean in 2002 — both as captain and batsman. To quote former English Test cricketer Ron Headley, 'Carl was the most suitable captain after Jimmy [Adams]. He is competitive, knowledgeable — a good man manager.'

Although selected for the first Test in Guyana against Steve Waugh's Australians in April 2003, Hooper withdrew from the team, indicating his disappointment at losing the captaincy. With so many ups and downs, eclipses and full moons, his Test record is creditable, if not outstanding. In a chequered hide-and-seek career, he scored 5762 runs at 36.47 with 13 centuries (highest score 233) in 102 Tests. He also took 114 wickets at 49.43 (with five wickets in an innings four times, the best being 5 for 26 *v.* Sri Lanka at St Vincents in 1996–97) and 115 catches.

Nicknamed 'Sir Carl' by his native Guyanese and Bajan 'subjects,' Carl Hooper has been described as everything from a future Viv Richards to an oxymoronic great under-achiever. Few cricketers have had such a mixture of good and bad press as Hooper. He has been praised lavishly and scorned just as intensely.

Rating for 100th Test: 1/10.

28 The 90-Plus Test Club

Apart from the 27 Test centurions featured in the book, 12 have played 90 to 99 Tests each, as at 15 May 2003. They are:

Player	*Country*	*Tests*
Mohammad Azharuddin	India	99
Curtly Ambrose	West Indies	98
Rodney Marsh	Australia	96
Alan Knott	England	95
Brian Lara	West Indies	94*
Garry Sobers	West Indies	93
Arvinda de Silva	Sri Lanka	93
Arjuna Ranatunga	Sri Lanka	93
Glenn McGrath	Australia	93*
Godfrey Evans	England	91
Gundappa Viswanath	India	91
Bob Willis	England	90

* = Current players who may play more Tests.

It is possible that Lara and McGrath may graduate to the 100-Test Club before the end of 2003. South Africa's opening batsman Gary Kirsten has played 89 Tests to date and Pakistan's fast bowler Waqar Younis 87, and they may possibly reach their century.

The first cricketer to play 90 Test was England's flamboyant wicket-keeper batsman Godfrey Evans. Arguably, he was the best wicket-keeper the game has known and the most charismatic. He played his 91st and last Test against India at Lord's in June 1959. He made a naught, took two catches and stumped one as England won by eight wickets. He completed 219 dismissals (173 catches and 46 stumpings), both his catches and dismissal figures were Test record

Three centurions — Tendulkar drives, Warne dives and Healy waits during the 1998 Chennai Test. *(Courtesy G.E. Features)*

then. After this Test he lost his place to Roy Swetman. Evans was then 37 and Swetman was brought in for team building for the future. Evans promptly retired. Colin Cowdrey played in Evans' final Test which was Cowdrey's 36th. He went on to become Test cricket's first centurion nine years later. To the next generation, Evans will be remembered as the cheery character with mutton-chop whiskers. He became the resident cricket expert for bookmakers Ladbrokes, reassessing the odds at every twist and turn of a Test match. He died on 3 May 1999, aged 78. Always a humorist, he said that his cherished CBE stood for Crumpet Before Evensong!

It was a bookmaker, an illegal one, who led to the 'demise' of Mohammad Azharuddin's cricket career after he had played 99 Tests for India. Azhar's Test career had a fairytale beginning (so far he is the only one to score a century in each of his first three Tests, against England in 1984–85) and a nightmarish finish. In the second and final Test, his 99th, against South Africa in Bangalore, the 37-year-old Indian scored 102 in the second innings, studded with 13 fours and two sixes, out of India's total of 250. His century was a dazzling innings replete with glorious drives and wristy onside strokes which did not save India from an innings defeat and a 0-2 series loss.

No-one had an inkling then that this would be Azhar's swan song.

After the South Africa – India series, the Hansie Cronje match-fixing scandal came out in the open and rocked the cricket world. During investigations in South Africa, Cronje stated that Azhar had introduced him to the bookmaker who had offered him the bribe. Azhar denied the allegation strongly but later admitted to certain acts of indiscretion. He was banned from playing any form of cricket. What a way to go after scoring 6215 runs at 45.03 with 22 Test hundreds.

Why did the others call it a day when so close to a landmark of 100 Tests? Rod Marsh was in good form in his 96th and final Test (against Pakistan in Sydney in January 1984). This Test will be remembered for being a joint swan song for Australian legends Greg Chappell (7110 runs and 122 catches in 87 Tests), Dennis Lillee (355 wickets in 70 Tests) and Marsh (355 dismissals, 95 of them caught off Lillee's bowling, in 96 Tests). Lillee and Chappell had announced their retirement during the Test and Marsh followed a little later. Just as for the Three Musketeers, it was one for all and all for one for the fabulous Aussie trio.

Fast bowler Ambrose was too tired after his 98th Test and cared little for figures. Indeed he was proud of his 405 Test wickets at 20.99 but to steam in to bowl at 145 to 150 kmh day in and day out was a bit much for a 37-year-old.

India's elegant stroke-player Viswanath was also not a stats-hog. He was pleased with his 6080 runs at 41.93 in 91 Tests and he retired a week before his 34th birthday, perhaps unaware that he was only nine Tests short of a landmark. In the past, cricketers were not made aware of milestones about to be reached as they are today. Also, in general, playing 100 Tests does not appear to be a big deal for most cricketers, judging from interviews I had with some of the centurions, or from reading their autobiographies/biographies/ghosted autobiographies/ tour diaries. Only Ian Healy, to my knowledge, has gone in detail about his 100th Test in his autobiography, *Hands and Heals*, and that was because his father had died a few days before this landmark mach. On interviewing the players on their 100th Test emotions, their eyes twinkled but no-one seemed all that excited. 'It was a proud moment but I did not feel any different than usual as I went out to bat/field,' was a prototype answer.

Here are the Test figures of the 12 cricketers who have played 90 to 99 Tests:

Player	*Country*	*Tests*	*Runs*	*Av.*	*Wkts*	*Aver.*	*Cat.*	*St.*
M. Azharuddin	Ind.	99	6215	45.03	0	–	105	–
C.E.L. Ambrose	W.I.	98	1439	12.40	405	20.99	18	–
R.W. Marsh	Aus.	96	3633	26.51	0	–	343	12
A.P.E. Knott	Eng.	95	4389	32.75	–	–	250	19
B.C. Lara*	W.I.	94	8105	50.34	0	–	120	–
G.S. Sobers	W.I.	93	8032	57.78	235	34.03	109	–
P.A. de Silva	S.L.	93	6361	42.97	29	41.65	43	–
A. Ranatunga	S.L.	93	5105	35.69	16	65.00	47	–
G.D. McGrath*	Aus.	93	450	6.62	425	21.68	29	–
G.R. Viswanath	Ind.	91	6080	41.93	1	46.00	63	–
T.G. Evans	Eng.	91	2439	20.49	–	–	173	46
R.G.D. Willis	Eng	90	840	11.50	325	25.20	39	–

* = Current players

As mentioned above, Test cricket was almost 92 years old when Cowdrey became the first to play 100 Tests, in Test number 639. Thirty-five years since Cowdrey's pioneering feat, 26 more have played 100 Tests each (with two more, Lara and McGrath, on the trail). Significantly, however, a little over 1000 Tests have been played since 1968, at 28.5 Tests a calendar year. Compare this with seven Tests per year before 1968. In other words, Tests have been played at four times greater frequency since 1968.

Apart from the ballooning of the number of Tests, there is also the money factor since 1977. Kerry Packer's involvement in cricket made Test cricketers well-paid professionals and made a significant improvement in their lifestyle and bank balance. No wonder top cricketers are disinclined to retire until given a push.

As shown in the Table below, only two cricketers had played 100 Tests from 1877 to 1983. Then the prevalence increased; two played their 100th Test in 1984, four in 1988, two in 1989, one each in 1990, 1991, 1992, 1993 and 1995, five in 1998, four in 2000 and three in 2002. The book may need updating every two to three years!

Sachin Tendulkar holding the Border–Gavaskar Trophy, appropriately flanked by celebrated centurions Allan Border and Sunil Gavaskar. *(Courtesy G.E. Features)*

Cricketers Who Have Played More Than 100 Tests

Player	*For*	*Against*	*Venue*	*Year*
M.C. Cowdrey	Eng.	Aus.	Birmingham	July 1968
G. Boycott	Eng.	Aus.	Lord's	July 1981
C.H. Lloyd	W.I.	Aus.	Jamaica	April–May 1984
S.M. Gavaskar	Ind.	Pak.	Lahore	October 1984
D.I. Gower	Eng.	W.I.	Leeds	July 1988
I.V.A. Richards	W.I.	Aus.	Brisbane	November 1988
D.B. Vengsarkar	Ind.	N.Z.	Mumbai	November 1988
A.R. Border	Aus.	W.I.	Melbourne	December 1988
Kapil Dev, N.	Ind.	Pak.	Karachi	November 1989
Javed Miandad	Pak.	Ind.	Lahore	December 1989
C.G. Greenidge	W.I.	Eng.	Antigua	April 1990
D.L. Haynes	W.I.	Eng.	Notts	July 1991
I.T. Botham	Eng.	N.Z.	Wellington	February 1992
G.A. Gooch	Eng.	Ind.	Kolkata	January 1993
D.C. Boon	Aus.	W.I.	Port-of-Spain	April 1995
S.R. Waugh	Aus.	S.A.	Sydney	January 1998
I.A. Healy	Aus.	S.A.	Adelaide	Jan–Feb 1998
C.A. Walsh	W.I.	Eng.	Georgetown	Feb–March 1998
M.A. Taylor	Aus.	Eng.	Brisbane	November 1998
Salim Malik	Pak.	Zim.	Lahore	December 1998
M.E. Waugh	Aus.	Ind.	Sydney	January 2000
M.A. Atherton	Eng.	W.I.	Manchester	August 2000
A.J. Stewart	Eng.	W.I.	Manchester	August 2000
Wasim Akram	Pak.	Eng.	Faisalabad	Nov–Dec 2000
S.K. Warne	Aus.	S.A.	Cape Town	March 2002
S.R. Tendulkar	Ind.	Eng.	The Oval	September 2002
C.L. Hooper	W.I.	Ind.	Mumbai	October 2002

Appearing in 100 Test matches places a cricketer in an elite group. These are men who have been kicked and garlanded, worshipped and booed, but have stayed and delivered time and again for their country, overcoming daunting odds along the way. It is an overwhelming achievement, focusing on their skill, commitment, fitness and strength of character.

The 1996 Australian World Cup team in the Indian subcontinent had five future100 Tests men: Shane Warne and Mark Waugh (standing), Steve Waugh, captain Mark Taylor and Ian Healy (sitting).

Statistics

Figures accurate to 15 May 2003
(Compiled with the help of C. Keshava Murthy)

Performance of Players in their 100th Tests

	Player	For	Batting 1st Ings	Batting 2nd Ings	Bowling 1st Ings	Bowling 2nd Ings	Cat./ St.
1	Cowdrey, M.C.	Eng.	**104**	–	–	–	0
2	Boycott, G.	Eng.	17	**60**	–	–	0
3	Lloyd, C.H.	W.I.	20	–	–	–	0
4	Gavaskar, S.M.	Ind.	48	37	–	–	3
5	Gower, D.I.	Eng.	13	2	–	–	1
6	Richards, I.V.A.	W.I.	**68**	–	0-01	0-26	2
7	Vengsarkar, D.B.	Ind.	25	0	–	–	2
8	Border, A.R.	Aus.	0	20	–	0-00	3
9	Kapil Dev	Ind.	**55**	–	4-69	3-82	0
10	Javed Miandad	Pak.	**145**	–	–	–	1
11	Greenidge, C.G.	W.I.	**149**	–	–	–	1
12	Haynes, D.L.	W.I.	18	**57***	–	–	0
13	Botham, I.T.	Eng.	15	1	1-53	2-23	1
14	Gooch, G.A.	Eng.	17	18	–	–	1
15	Boon, D.C.	Aus.	18	9	–	–	0
16	Waugh, S.R.	Aus.	**85**	–	0-10	–	1
17	Healy, I.A.	Aus.	1	10	–	–	2 / 1
18	Walsh, C.A.	W.I.	3*	0	2-47	3-25	1
19	Taylor, M.A.	Aus.	46	0	–	–	0
20	Salim Malik	Pak.	2	–	–	–	1
21	Waugh, M.E.	Aus.	32	–	–	–	4
22	Atherton, M.A.	Eng.	1	28	–	–	0
23	Stewart, A.J.	Eng.	**105**	–	–	–	2
24	Wasim Akram	Pak.	1	4*	1-69	0-13	0
25	Warne, S.K.	Aus.	**63**	15*	2-70	**6-161**	1
26	Tendulkar, S.R.	Ind.	**54**	-	0-04	-	0
27	Hooper, C.L.	W.I.	23	1	1-40	-	1

Note: Figures in bold indicate individual score of more than 50 runs or more than five wickets per innings.

- Colin Cowdrey, Javed Miandad, Gordon Greenidge and Alec Stewart scored centuries in their 100th Test.
- Javed Miandad and Gordon Greenidge had also scored centuries in their Test debut.
- Shane Warne is the only player to take five wickets in an innings (6-161) in his 100th Test.

Master bat Sachin Tendulkar and Master Blaster Viv Richards together, hand in glove, mobile in pocket. (*Sportstar*, India)

Batting and Fielding Figures of 100 Test Men

(in alphabetical order)

Player	*For*	*Tests*	*Ings*	*NO*	*Runs*	*HS*	*Ave*	*100s*	*50s*	*0s*	*90s*	*Cat*	*St.*
Atherton, M.A.	Eng.	115	212	7	7728	185*	37.70	16	46	20	5	83	–
Boon, D.C.	Aus.	107	190	20	7422	200	43.66	21	32	16	5	99	–
Border, A.R.	Aus.	156	265	44	11,174	205	50.56	27	63	11	3	156	–
Botham, I.T.	Eng.	102	161	6	5200	208	33.55	14	22	14	0	120	–
Boycott, G.	Eng.	108	193	23	8114	246*	47.73	22	42	10	6	33	–
Cowdrey, M.C.	Eng.	114	188	15	7624	182	44.07	22	38	9	4	120	–
Gavaskar, S.M.	Ind.	125	214	16	10,122	236*	51.12	34	45	12	5	108	–
Gooch, G.A.	Eng.	118	215	6	8900	333	42.58	20	46	13	3	103	–
Gower, D.I.	Eng.	117	204	18	8231	215	44.25	18	39	7	2	74	–
Greenidge, C.G.	W.I.	108	185	16	7558	226	44.72	19	34	11	6	96	–
Haynes, D.L.	W.I.	116	202	25	7487	184	42.30	18	39	10	3	65	–
Healy, I.A.	Aus.	119	182	23	4356	161*	27.40	4	22	18	1	366	29
Hooper, C.L.	W.I.	102	173	15	5762	233	36.47	13	27	13	1	115	–
Javed Miandad	Pak.	124	189	21	8832	280*	52.57	23	43	6	4	93	1
Kapil Dev, N.	Ind.	131	184	15	5248	163	31.05	8	27	16	2	64	–
Lloyd, C.H.	W.I.	110	175	14	7515	242*	46.68	19	39	4	3	90	–
Richards, I.V.A.	W.I.	121	182	12	8540	291	50.24	24	45	10	3	122	–
Salim Malik	Pak.	103	154	22	5768	237	43.70	15	29	12	2	65	–
Stewart, A.J.	Eng.	126	225	21	8187	190	40.13	15	43	13	2	247	13
Taylor, M.A.	Aus.	104	186	13	7525	334*	43.50	19	40	5	4	157	–
Tendulkar, S.R.	Ind.	105	169	16	8811	217	57.59	31	35	10	5	68	–
Vengsarkar, D.B.	Ind.	116	185	22	6868	166	42.13	17	35	15	4	78	–
Walsh, C.A.	W.I.	132	185	61	936	30	7.55	0	0	43	0	29	–
Warne, S.K.	Aus.	107	146	13	2238	99	16.83	0	8	27	1	86	–
Wasim Akram	Pak.	104	147	19	2898	257*	22.64	3	7	17	0	44	–
Waugh, M.E.	Aus.	128	209	17	8029	153*	41.82	20	47	19	2	181	–
Waugh, S.R.	Aus.	160	249	43	10,265	200	49.83	30	46	21	10	109	–

Note:

- Steve Waugh has played most Tests (160) and scored most nineties (10).
- Allan Border has played most innings (265), scored most runs (11,174) and most fifties (63).
- Mark Taylor has scored the highest individual score (334 not out *v.* Pakistan at Peshawar in 1998–99).

•Graham Gooch is the only one to score a triple century and a century (333 and 123) in the same Test, *v.* India at Lord's in 1990. His 456 runs is the highest aggregate by a player in one Test.
•Sachin Tendulkar has the best batting average (57.59).
•Sunil Gavaskar has scored most centuries (34).
•Ian Healy has taken most catches (366) and made most stumpings (29).
•Mark Waugh has accepted most catches (181) among non wicket-keepers.
•Courtney Walsh has remained not out most times (61) and made most ducks (43).

Bowling Figures of 100 Test Men

(in alphabetical order)

Player	*For*	*Tests*	*Balls*	*Mdns*	*Runs*	*Wkts*	*Ave*	*Best*	*5w/i*	*10w/T*
Atherton, M.A.	Eng.	115	408	12	302	2	151.00	1-20	–	–
Boon, D.C.	Aus.	107	36	3	14	0	–	0-0	–	–
Border, A.R.	Aus.	156	4009	199	1525	39	39.10	7-46	2	1
Botham, I.T.	Eng.	102	21,815	788	10,878	383	28.40	8-34	27	4
Boycott, G.	Eng.	108	944	45	382	7	54.57	3-47	–	–
Cowdrey, M.C.	Eng.	114	119	0	104	0	–	0-1	–	–
Gavaskar, S.M.	Ind.	125	380	15	206	1	206.0	1-34	–	–
Gooch, G.A.	Eng.	118	2655	122	1069	23	46.48	3-39	–	–
Gower, D.I.	Eng.	117	36	0	20	1	20.00	1-1	–	–
Greenidge, C.G.	W.I.	108	26	3	4	0	–	0-0	–	–
Haynes, D.L.	W.I.	116	18	0	8	1	8.00	1-2	–	–
Healy, I.A.	Aus.	119								
Hooper, C.L.	W.I.	102	13,788	531	5635	114	49.43	5-26	4	–
Javed Miandad	Pak.	124	1470	32	682	17	40.12	3-74	–	–
Kapil Dev, N.	Ind.	131	27,740	1060	12,867	434	29.65	9-83	23	2
Lloyd, C.H.	W.I.	110	1716	75	622	10	62.20	2-13	–	–
Richards, I.V.A.	W.I.	121	5170	203	1964	32	61.38	2-17	–	–
Salim Malik	Pak.	103	734	20	414	5	82.80	1-3	–	–
Stewart, A.J.	Eng.	126	20	0	13	0	–	0-5	–	–
Taylor, M.A.	Aus.	104	42	3	26	1	26.00	1-11	–	–
Tendulkar, S.R.	Ind.	105	2286	63	1220	27	45.19	3-10	–	–
Vengsarkar, D.B.	Ind.	116	47	1	36	0	–	0-3	–	–
Walsh, C.A.	W.I.	132	30,019	1145	12,688	519	24.45	7-37	22	3
Warne, S.K.	Aus.	107	29,876	1416	12,624	491	25.71	8-71	23	6
Wasim Akram	Pak.	104	22,627	871	9779	414	23.62	7-119	25	5
Waugh, M.E.	Aus.	128	4853	171	2429	59	41.17	5-40	1	–
Waugh, S.R.	Aus.	158	7433	320	3285	91	36.10	5-28	3	–

(Ian Healy did not bowl)

Note:
•Courtney Walsh bowled most balls (30,019), took mostwickets(519)
•Shane Warne bowled most maidens (1416) and took 10 wickets in a Test most times (six).
•Kapil Dev conceded most runs (12,867) and had the best figures in an innings (9-83, *v.* West Indies at Ahmedabad in 1983–84). He is the only one to capture nine wickets in a Test innings when captaining his country.

•Ian Botham took five wickets in an innings most times (27).
•Wasim Akram had the best bowling average (23.62, qualification, a minmum 50 balls bowled).

Age, Runs Scored and Wickets Taken at the Start of the Players' 100th Test

Player	*Yrs*	*Days*	*For*	*Runs*	*Wkts*	*v.*	*Test*	*Series*	*Venue*
Tendulkar, S.R.	29	134	Ind.	8351	27	Eng.	4th	2002	The Oval
Kapil Dev, N.	30	313	Ind.	4087	347	Pak.	1st	1989–90	Karachi
Gower, D.I.	31	111	Eng.	6985	1	W.I.	4th	1988	Leeds
Atherton, M.A.	32	133	Eng.	6713	2	W.I.	3rd	2000	Manchester
Javed Miandad	32	172	Pak.	7549	17	Ind.	3rd	1989–90	Lahore
Warne, S.K.	32	176	Aus.	1974	436	S.A.	2nd	2001–02	Cape Town
Waugh, S.R.	32	214	Aus.	6203	85	S.A.	2nd	1997–98	Sydney
Vengsarkar, D.B.	32	232	Ind.	6331	0	N.Z.	2nd	1988–89	Mumbai
Border, A.R.	33	150	Aus.	7650	16	W.I.	3rd	1988–89	Melbourne
Healy, I.A.	33	275	Aus.	3730	0	S.A.	3rd	1997–98	Adelaide
Taylor, M.A.	34	24	Aus.	7297	1	Eng.	1st	1998–99	Brisbane
Boon, D.C.	34	113	Aus.	7067	0	W.I.	3rd	1994–95	Port-of-Spain
Wasim Akram	34	179	Pak.	2810	408	Eng.	2nd	2000–01	Faisalabad
Waugh, M.E.	34	214	Aus.	6371	50	Ind.	3rd	1999–00	Sydney
Gavaskar, S.M.	35	99	Ind.	8394	1	Pak.	1st	1984–85	Lahore
Walsh, C.A.	35	120	W.I.	791	362	Eng.	4th	1997–98	Georgetown
Haynes, D.L.	35	139	W.I.	6411	1	Eng.	3rd	1991	Nottingham
Cowdrey, M.C.	35	200	Eng.	6940	0	Aus.	3rd	1968	Birmingham
Salim Malik	35	238	Pak.	5639	5	Zim.	2nd	1998–99	Lahore
Hooper, C.L.	35	298	W.I.	5638	110	Ind.	1st	2002–03	Mumbai
Botham, I.T.	36	74	Eng.	5176	380	N.Z.	3rd	1991–92	Wellington
Richards, I.V.A.	36	256	W.I.	7268	28	Aus.	1st	1988–89	Brisbane
Stewart, A.J.	37	117	Eng.	6733	0	W.I.	3rd	2000	Manchester
Greenidge, C.G.	38	346	W.I.	6985	0	Eng.	5th	1989–90	St John's
Gooch, G.A.	39	190	Eng.	7573	22	Ind.	1st	1992–93	Kolkata
Lloyd, C.H.	39	241	W.I.	6884	10	Aus.	5th	1983–84	Kingston
Boycott, G.	40	254	Eng.	7441	7	Aus.	2nd	1981	Lord's

Note:
•Sachin Tendulkar was the youngest to appear in his 100th Test.
•Geoff Boycott was the oldest to appear in his 100th Test.
•Mark Waugh of Australia holds the record for reaching the milestone of 100 Tests in the quickest time, 8 years 342 days.
•Sunil Gavaskar had made most runs (8394) and Shane Warne had taken most wickets (436) on the morning of their 100th Test.

Bibliography

Books

Atherton, Mike, *Opening Up: My Autobiography*, Hodder & Stoughton, London, 2000.

Boon, David (with A. Mark Thomas), *Boon, In the Firing Line: An Autobiography*, Pan Macmillan Publishers, Sydney, 1993.

Border, Allan, *Beyond Ten Thousand: My Life Story*, Swan Publishing, Nedlands, WA, 1993.

Boycott, Geoff, *Boycott: The Autobiography*, Macmillan, London, 1987.

Cowdrey, Colin, *MCC: The Autobiography of a Cricketer*, Hodder & Stoughton, London, 1976.

Eagar, Patrick, *Botham*, The Kingswood Press, Surrey, 1985.

Ezekiel, Gulu, *Sachin: The Story of World's Greatest Batsman*, Penguin Books, New Delhi, 2002.

Frindall, Bill (compiled), *The Wisden Book of Test Cricket, 1876–77 to 1977–78)*, Macdonald & Jane's, London, 1978.

Frindall, Bill (compiled), *The Wisden Book of Test Cricket, Vol. II, 1979–1994*, Headline Book Publishing, London, 1995.

Gavaskar, Sunil, *Sunny Days: Sunil Gavaskar's Own Story*, Rupa & Co., Kolkata, 1976.

Gavaskar, Sunil, *Idols*, Rupa & Co., Kolkata, 1983.

Gooch, Graham (with Frank Keating), *Gooch: My Autobiography*, CollinsWillow, London, 1995.

Gower, David, and Alan Lee, *David Gower: With Time to Spare*, Ward Lock, London, 1980.

Greenidge, Gordon (with Patrick Symes), *Gordon Greenidge: The Man in the Middle*, David & Charles, Devon, 1980.

Haigh, Gideon, *The Border Years*, Text, Melbourne, 1994.

Healy, Ian, *Hands and Heals: The Autobiography*, HarperSports, Sydney, 2000.

Imran Khan (with Patrick Murphy), *Imran: The Autobiography of Imran Khan*, Pelham Books, London, 1983.

Indian Cricket, Kasturi and Sons, Chennai, many editions.

Knight, James, *Mark Waugh: The Biography*, HarperSports, Sydney, 2002.

Lloyd, Clive (with Tony Cozier), *Living for Cricket*, Stanley Paul, Hutchinson Publishing Group, London, 1980.

Martin-Jenkins, Christopher M., *World Cricketers: A Biographical Dictionary*, Oxford University Press, Oxford, 1996.

Meher-Homji, Kersi, *Hat-Tricks*, Kangaroo Press, Sydney, 1995.

Meher-Homji, Kersi, *The Waugh Twins*, Kangaroo Press/Simon & Schuster, Sydney, 1998.

Meher-Homji, Kersi, *Dramatic Debuts and Swan Songs*, ABC Books, Sydney, 2001.

Rehmatullah, A. Aziz, et al., *Calendar Year Kings*, A. Aziz Rehmatullah, Karachi, 2002.

Richards, Vivian (with Bob Harris), *Sir Vivian: The Definitive Autobiography*, Michael Joseph, London, 2000.

Sobers, Garry (with Bob Harris), *Garry Sobers: My Autobiography*, Headline Book Publishing, London, 2002.
Warne, Shane (with Richard Hobson), *Shane Warne: My Autobiography*, Hodder & Stoughton, London, 2001.
Waugh, Steve, *Never Satisfied: The Diary of a Record-Breaking Year*, HarperSports, Sydney, 2000.
Wisden Cricketers' Almanack, John Wisden and Co., Guilford, Surrey, many editions.
Wisden Cricketers' Almanack Australia, 1998 – 2002–03, Hardie Grant Books, Melbourne

Magazines/Dailies

ABC Cricket Book (Aus.)
Allan's Australian Cricket Annual (Aus.)
The Australian (Aus.)
The Cricket Statistician (U.K.)
The Cricketer (U.K.)
Daily Telegraph (Aus.)
The Indian Down Under (Aus.)
Inside Edge (Aus.)
Mid-Day (Ind.)
Sportstar (Ind.)
Sportsworld (Ind.)
Sun-Herald (Aus.)
Sydney Morning Herald (Aus.)
The Times (U.K.)
Wisden Cricket Monthly (U.K.)

Websites

CricInfo.com
Sifysports/ khel.com

Index